# Indian
## MOTORCYCLE
# PHOTOGRAPHIC HISTORY

Jerry Hatfield

Motorbooks International
Publishers & Wholesalers

First published in 1993 by Motorbooks
International Publishers & Wholesalers,
PO Box 2, 729 Prospect Avenue, Osceola, WI
54020 USA

Library of Congress Cataloging-in-Publication
Data

Hatfield, Jerry H.
    Indian motorcycle photographic history /
Jerry Hatfield.
        p.   cm.
    Includes index.
    ISBN 0-87938-736-X
    1. Indian motorcycle—History.   I. Title.
TL448.I5H38    1993
629.227'5—dc20                93-24760

Printed and bound in the United States of
America

**On the front cover:** The 1938 Indian Four owned
by Chuck Sterne. The engine was restored by
Dennis Young and the chassis by Jerry Greer's
Indian Engineering. The motorcycle was featured
in the August 1993 edition of Don Emde's
*Motorcycle Collector Magazine. Nick Cedar*

**On the frontispiece:** Goodyear sales
representative Dave Kinnie poses with Indian
factory rider Roy Artley at one of the Marion road
races, circa 1919. *Kinnie/Cox*

**On the title pages:** Los Angeles Stadium
motordrome, 1912. *Bob Smith*

# Contents

# Dedication

To Jimmy Hill, for his long service to Indian and his foresight to save Indian photographic history . . .

. . . and in memory of Earl Bentley, for his love of Indians reflected in restorations and photos.

# Preface

A survey of American homes in the late 1920s found Indian to be the most widely recognized name in motorcycling. In fact, many people—women of the so-called upper class, for example—could name only *one* motorcycle, which invariably was Indian. Harley-Davidson? Who was that?

For most of the first twenty-five years of the twentieth century, Indian was the world's largest-selling motorcycle and held the most speed records. Of all American brands, only Indian had won the Isle of Man Tourist Trophy (TT), the premier motorcycle race of the world. Only the rider of an Indian had been personally congratulated by the president of the United States for a racing victory. Sixty percent of the nation's population was policed by Indian motorcycles. Yet, all this glory became undone by the 1950s because of a succession of management mistakes.

When all logic called for closing the doors, time and again there arose the unmuted cry of support from Indian fans, filled with love for their scarlet steeds of steel. Perhaps no product before or since has enjoyed stronger customer support.

The beat goes on. The Indian motorcycle company—never mind its various formal names—failed in the economic sense. But the company was a roaring success in the larger sense: How many companies create something so indestructible that brings so much joy to so many people over the generations? These Indian motorcycles, these enduring examples of artistry in metal, continue to caress our eyes and ears, to bring back memories, to excite our imaginations, to pump up our passion for living.

The author, on his 1938 Indian Four with Vard forks. Restoration by Max Bubeck.

# Acknowledgments

I am indebted to many, without whose help and encouragement this book would not have been possible. Enormous contributions were made by former Indian staffer Jimmy Hill, who had the foresight to save many Indian archives photographs, and by the late Earl Bentley who made many outstanding copy photos from archive originals. In fact, Earl launched this book by offering the loan of his copy negatives—I never would have begun the book without Earl's help. Jimmy and his late wife Florence also welcomed me to their home for further photo copying.

Original Indian archives negatives are a historian's gold. Former Indian advertising manager Bob Finn entrusted me with his extraordinary and irreplaceable negatives, for which I'm deeply grateful.

I'm touched by the generosity of Russ Cox, who donated the D. O. Kinnie photograph collection. This historical treasure chest has seen use in this book and will be used in my future writings over the years.

My friends Matt and Peg Keevers hosted two visits to Springfield, Massachusetts. Acting as intermediary to arrange visits with Jimmy Hill and Fred Marsh, Matt also has been my personal cheerleader over the years. His bubbly personality made him a natural choice as former Indian advertising manager.

England was a surprising source of many Indian archives photographs. Launched in 1903, the British magazine *The Motor Cycle* was joined shortly thereafter by *Motor Cycling*. The two magazines provided weekly reporting of motorcycling since the first decade of the twentieth century. Because of the importance of the British market, Indian sent many archives photos to these magazines. The photograph collections of *The Motor Cycle* and *Motor Cycling* now are copyrighted by EMAP Publications. I thank Brian Woolley for researching my needs, Phillip Tooth for assisting in copying photographs, and EMAP Publications for permission to use this material.

Rare inside views of the Indian company are provided by the E. Paul du Pont papers, donated by the du Pont family to the Henry Ford Museum in Dearborn, Michigan. My appreciation goes to Alexis du Pont and to the du Pont family for their generosity, and to the museum staff for permission to use the materials and for their assistance. I'm also grateful to Don Doody, who made me aware of the du Pont papers, and for his other assistance.

Ted and Brenda Buhl hosted a research visit. Woody Carson donated a photo and *Cycle World* permitted the use of a photo. Clyde Earl made available numerous historic photos. Professional photographer John O. L. Finucan permitted the use of photos. Jeff Grigsby provided a photo. My wife Ella Hatfield contributed a photo. The late Bill Hoecker arranged for my purchase of an Indian dealers sales kit, which was the source of several photos. Elmer Lower, Pete Sink, and Howard Wagner provided photo assistance with their outstanding restorations. Fred Marsh shared his photos. Charles and Esta Mathos of the Indian Motocycle Museum encouraged me. Art McMullin provided information. Fellow motorcycle historian Bruce Palmer loaned photos of military Indians. Paul Pearce helped me with photos. Jim Anderson coordinated the photo requirement for his motorcycle. Bob Shingler provided information. George and Milli Yarocki hosted a visit and shared their extensive literature resources.

Over the years, several people assisted me with earlier books. Their contributions either debut or find reuse in this publication. These long-run helpers were: the late Dewey Bonkrud, Max Bubeck, Ian Campbell, my late father-in-law Bill Ellington, George Hays, Bobby Hill, Geoff Hockley, Sam Hotton, the late Hap Jones, the late Maldwyn Jones, Ed Kretz, Sr., the late Fred Markwick, Harold Mathewson, the late Emmett Moore, H. J. Norman, the late Sam Pierce, Dick and Rita Sanchez, Bob Smith, Chuck Vernon, and Stephen Wright.

Finally, I mention again my friend Max Bubeck. He undertook the restoration of my 1938 Indian Four when the writing of three successive books prevented me from turning wrenches. Thanks, Max, for giving me the time I needed and for building me a better-than-new Indian Four.

# 1882–1895

## *Springfield Wheels*

In 1882, sixteen-year-old George M. Hendee of Springfield, Massachusetts, took his first ride on a penny farthing bicycle. Hendee was captivated and immediately entered the bicycle racing movement.

**George Hendee, circa 1884**
Amateur bicycle racing champion.

The following year, the American championships at Springfield drew 32,000 fans, some from as far away as the Pacific coast. Few, if any, American sporting events had ever enjoyed such attendance; special trainloads of fans arrived from as far away as Chicago. Among other events, the huge crowd watched Hendee win the One-Mile National Championship for amateurs.

Hendee won four more amateur one-mile championships during the years 1884 through 1891, including a streak of three consecutive wins that awarded him permanent possession of the championship medal. He also won the Two-, Five-, and Ten-Mile National Championships for amateurs during this span of years. From 1883 through 1891, Hendee entered 309 amateur contests, winning 302 and losing only seven!

By 1892, the safety bicycle, with two equally sized wheels and rear-wheel drive, began to catch on. Hendee forsook his amateur status and mastery of the high-wheel bicycle and began racing safety bicycles on the East Coast's board track venues, known as velodromes.

Although trains were increasing in number, they didn't go everywhere. Thus, horses provided door-to-door personal transportation for millions of Americans: some 25 million horses were at work all over North America in the 1890s. The safety bicycle's popularity was exploding, with hundreds of thousands of riders using it as a mode of transportation.

To the unimaginative, leg power seemed forever entrenched in the world of personal transportation. Yet, it did not require a great deal of imagination to consider the possibility of self-propelled, steam-powered vehicles someday chugging along the roadways. All that was needed were a few ingenious inventors with both dreams and know-how.

The practical dreamers didn't limit themselves to steam engines, however. Over the quiet streets of Springfield, local inventor J. Frank Duryea drove the first successful American gasoline-powered automobile. The year was 1893,

and Henry Ford's first car was still three years away.

But while this new self-propelled four-wheeler may have been seen as the wave of the future, the safety bicycle was the vehicle of the present. So, in 1895, George Hendee retired from bicycle racing to begin manufacturing bicycles. In the same year, fellow Springfielder Frank Duryea won *The Chicago Times Herald* road race for self-propelled four-wheelers. In connection with the race, the *Times Herald* sponsored a contest to find a new name to replace the objectionable term "horseless carriage." The winning entry was "motocycle." The word stuck in Hendee's mind, to be called to duty some years later.

**Oscar Hedstrom pacer, 1899**
In November 1899, Oscar Hedstrom completed this machine for pacing bicycles. In January 1900, the Hedstrom pacer debuted in New York's Madison Square Garden. The success of the Hedstrom pacer led to the launching of the Indian motocycle. *Indian archives photo in the Jimmy Hill collection, copied by the late Earl Bentley*

*Chapter 1*

# 1901–1908

## *The Motocycles*

In 1900, George Hendee supported bicycle racing for both personal and business reasons. Record-setting was important in the bicycle game, and to challenge short-distance records, riders used one of the newly introduced motor-driven bicycles as a wind breaker. Dissatisfied with the crude motor pacers in use at the Springfield Coliseum and having heard of a much improved pacer in New York, Hendee convinced the builder, Oscar Hedstrom, to bring his pacer to Springfield.

The Hedstrom machine lived up to Hendee's expectations, with its reliability and smooth, consistent performance. Hendee had food for thought. In January 1901, Hedstrom agreed to construct a prototype machine for Hendee. Only four months later, he rode the prototype forty-four miles from Middletown, Connecticut, to Springfield.

That first machine, which was shortly to be named the "Indian" and typecast as a motocycle, was stunning. Except for Hedstrom's earlier pacer, the few track pacers and home-built road models that preceded the Hedstrom road model relied on brute force and heavy weight more than cunning design. But the first Indian motocycle was an integrated vehicle, not just a beefed-up bicycle frame with a motor added as an afterthought. No part was larger or smaller than it should be. No unnecessary noises escaped it. The

Indian motocycle number 1 started repeatedly without hesitation, chugged quietly at a snail's pace, accelerated briskly to 30mph or so, and climbed steep hills with such reserve as to permit Hedstrom to deliberately slow down midway up the ascents and then reapply power for faster speed.

This machine was of such ingenious design, of such flawless construction, of such perfect proportion, that no rival would approach it during the all-important formative years of the American motorcycle industry.

The success of Oscar Hedstrom's initial Indian and George Hendee's prowess at attracting investors brought the Indian motocycle immediately into the limelight and established it as the industry leader. Meanwhile, Hedstrom continuously upgraded the Indian manufacturing facilities. Hendee and Hedstrom decided that engine manufacturing should be subcontracted while the Springfield plant expanded other capabilities, so Hedstrom supervised the transfer of motor manufacturing to the Aurora Automatic Machinery Company of Aurora, Illinois.

Racing success came immediately, and race reports were monotonous in their repetition of the word "Indian" when describing victories. Soon, that most sincere form of flattery, imitation, was abundant. Aurora, which had been given the right to sell off motor production in excess to Indian requirements, spawned not only their own Thor brand, but also a host of Indian imitators that were carbon copies of the real thing.

In 1905, Indian offered its first twin-cylinder machine to the public. The first Indian production racer followed in 1906.

Among the hundreds of Indian competition records and victories in these formative years, three stood out. In 1903, Oscar Hedstrom rode to a record 56mph at Ormond Beach, Florida, using a special loop-frame machine powered by the old Hedstrom pacing motor. In 1906, Indian set its first transcontinental record at the hands of Cleveland, Ohio, Indian dealer Louis Mueller, who lowered the mark to 31 1/2 days. In 1908, Jake De Rosier won a race on the Clinton, New Jersey, board track, the first board track in the nation built specifically for motorcycle racing. De Rosier's machine was based on an uncharacteristic frame for an Indian, the so-called loop frame that was shortly to displace the traditional bicycle-style diamond frame.

Indian enjoyed phenomenal growth from 1901 through 1908. Between 1905 and 1908, annual sales nearly tripled from 1,181 to 3,257. The machines that had done the job on the showroom floors were the classic diamond-frame singles and twins, and there was nothing wrong with their specifications.

Motorcyclists, however, had developed ideas about how motorcycles should look, and these ideas were more along the lines of the loop frame popularized by Harley-Davidson and others, but used by Indian only on a few record-setters.

**Oscar Hedstrom motocycle, 1901**
A photo appeared in the June 2, 1901, issue of the *Springfield Sunday Republican* showing the right side of the first "Hedstrom motor cycle," complete with the same-size fuel tank as shown in this left profile. The left profile was used by the Indian advertising department over the years and was claimed to be both a 1901 or 1902 model. The motor has two hold-down studs on the left side, instead of a single left-side stud as in later production models. *Indian archives via Bob Finn*

Fashion had to be served, so Indian was preparing a new line of loop-frame models for 1909. Although the company would continue to use the term motocycle for many years to come, the original diamond-frame motocycles and the charming era of low-speed pleasure cruising that they had brought about were victims not only of style but also of motorcyclists' unceasing craving for faster speeds. Thus, as 1908 came to a close, motocycling in its truest sense came to a close as well.

**Oscar Hedstrom, circa 1901**
Oscar Hedstrom and the Indian motocycle that the company long represented as the first Indian. The tank was larger than shown in the 1901 publicity photos, however, so this could be an early example rather than the very first machine. The small lever on the top of the frame tube progressively dropped the exhaust valve for starting, then advanced the ignition timing for speed control; the left-hand twist-grip throttle was used infrequently, for hills and other unusual conditions. *A. F. VanOrder via Bob Smith*

# HEDSTROM'S NEW MOTOR BICYCLE

*Which The Hendee Manufacturing
Company Is Likely to
Manufacture in This City*

Oscar Hedstrom, who became well known to frequenters of the Coliseum last season as a member of the riding team of Henshaw and Hedstrom, has just completed a motor bicycle for the Hendee Manufacturing Company of this city and the sample is now being shown here by Mr. Hedstrom. The new machine, of which illustrations are given, has numerous improvements that are expected to make it a desirable machine for general utility. It weighs but 75 pounds, has the same wheel base as the ordinary bicycle and has a tread of but 51/2 inches, or one-quarter of an inch more than the regular wheel. It is simple in mechanism, easy to operate and can be quickly controlled in case of emergency. It is also claimed by those interested that the machine can be run at a slower speed than other motor bicycles at present on the market. On tests the motor has shown efficiency when running at not more than four miles an hour and with the ordinary gear used for road riding fully 30 miles an hour can be attained. Mr. Hedstrom began working on the new model in February last and completed his first machine May 25. While the machine was built under the direction of the Hendee manufacturing company, it is planned to form a stock company in which only local capital will be interested and manufacture the machine in this city. George M. Hendee, who has been especially interested in the new invention, has already had offers for financing the new company if it were located in Connecticut, but it is believed that there is room for the enterprise in this city.

Mr. Hedstrom has won a reputation as one of the most practical motor tandem and cycle builders in the country, and he has done his best work in devising the present machine. He has put only the best material and careful workmanship into the new model. There are several new devices and eight patents have either been secured or applied for to cover practical improvements. The machine as it now stands gives its maker satisfaction, except perhaps for the muffler for deadening the sound of the explosions of gas. This does not at present secure the best results, and Mr. Hedstrom will provide some new arrangement.

*From* The Springfield Sunday Republican, *June 2, 1901*

**George Hendee, 1904**
Indian cofounder George Hendee astride a
motorcycle that company advertising once
claimed to be the first Indian. Not by a long shot
is this the first Indian, for it has the right-hand
twist-grip ignition control that was introduced

in 1904. Royal blue was the standard color on all
Indians from 1901 through 1911. Optional colors
were first offered in 1904, and included
vermillion, which was later called Indian red.
*Bob Finn*

**Indian motorcyclists, 1906**
Two Indian enthusiasts show the best in stylish motorcycle garb. The faded sign in the window brags about Indian endurance run performance. Endurance runs were more publicized than racing up to this time, although that was about to change. But wait—these are not ordinary tourists! They are Indian dealers Louis J. Mueller of Cleveland, Ohio (left) and George Holden of Springfield, Mass. (right). They were in route across North America, setting a record of 31 days, 12 hours, and 15 minutes for the 3,476 mile trip. Holden was the first Indian dealer. *EMAP archives*

**Walter Goerke, 1906**
Walter Goerke posing at Ormond Beach, Florida, aboard a special high-speed single-cylinder model based on the original Hedstrom pacer. The machine featured the pacer motor and parts from the pacer frame. Hedstrom rode this machine to a one-mile record of about 57mph. This example was probably the first loop-frame Indian. *EMAP archives*

**Indian twin, 1906-1908**
The first Indian twins were built in the autumn of 1904, but were not included in the sales catalog. The first advertised Indian twins were the 1906 racers similar to this 1908 example. Output was listed as 4hp, less than twice the output of the singles. Restoration by Stephen Wright.

**Indian twin, 1907**
The first cataloged Indian twins were the 1907 models. For 1907, the oil tank was moved behind the seat post and the fuel capacity was enlarged. This example was fitted with the new optional gear-driven primary drive. This was not a conventional gear drive; rather, it consisted of a driving wheel with small, cylindrical pins that engaged a conventional sprocket. *Bob Finn*

**T. K. Hastings,
Thousand Miles Trial, 1907**
The rider is T. K. "Teddy" Hastings, seen reporting in at a Scottish checkpoint in the British 1907 Thousand Miles Trial, which later became known as the International Six Days Trial. Looking over Hastings' shoulder is the Indian distributor for London, "Indian" Billy Wells. Hastings won the event and also earned the distinction of being the first American rider of an American machine to be entered in a British event. *Indian archives photo copied by Ian Campbell*

**Indian single, 1908**
The fork spring length was doubled on 1908 models, and a large mud flap was added to the front fender. This is the 19.3ci battery ignition model. Finishes were Royal blue, black, and Indian red, the latter a new term in the Indian lexicon. *Hill/Bentley*

**Indian factory, 1908**
In the Indian factory, a worker poses before connecting the rear cylinder head to the seat post. *Indian archives photo copied by Earl Bentley, loaned by George Yarocki*

**Indian factory, 1908**
A worker checks out motor operation, as can be seen by the spinning rear wheel. The fuel tank on this motorcycle had extra-cost lettering, reading, "The Hathaway Motor Company, Denver, Colorado." In the background, another single is being run up. *Bentley/Yarocki*

**Indian factory, 1908**
This technician is fitting cylinder heads to a batch of battery ignition 38.6ci, 633cc twins. The assembled motor behind him has the contact breaker points exposed, which distinguishes the battery ignition motors from the magneto ignition types. From the stock of parts on the workbench, he will later install push-pull rods and valve springs. *Bentley/Yarocki*

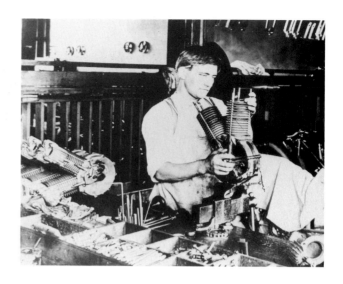

*Below*
**Indian twin, 1908**
Two sizes of twin-cylinder motors were offered in 1908. This is the smaller 38.6ci, 633cc model. Mechanical inlet valves, as shown here, were the new standard, but automatic (suction) inlet valves remained optional. *Hill/Bentley*

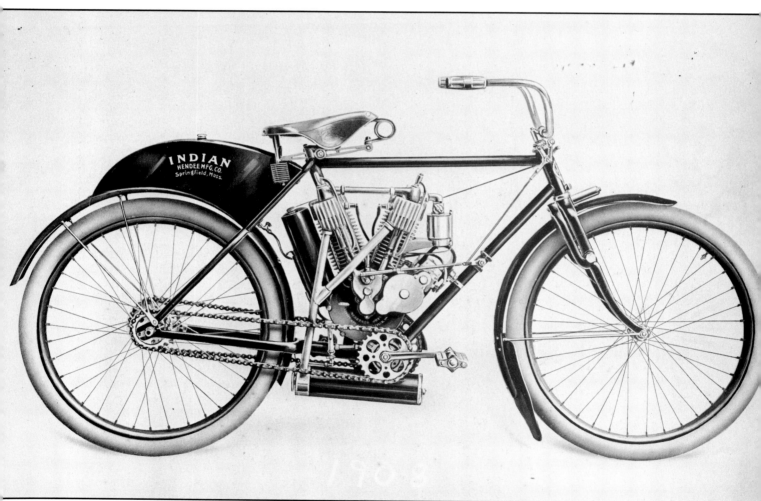

**Indian twin, 1908**
Left side of the 1908 twin.
*Hill/Bentley*

*Below*
**Accessories, 1908**
This 26.96ci, 442cc single
was equipped with several
accessories: longer handlebars,
torpedo tank, rear-mounted seat,
and magneto ignition, the latter
available on all models. The $40
optional magneto boosted the
model's price 18 percent.
*Hill/Bentley*

# Chapter 2

# 1909–1915

## *The F-Head Mainstream*

During the last half of the Hendee and Hedstrom era—from 1909 to 1915—Indian's Springfield factory virtually doubled in size. Production rose from 4,771 in 1909 to 32,000 in 1913, then declined to 25,000 and 21,000 in 1914 and 1915, respectively. Profits also grew handsomely, peaking in 1913 at $1.3 million, but remaining strong at $712,000 and $422,000 in 1914 and 1915, respectively. During this time, roughly $300 would purchase the best Indian motorcycle, whereas within a few years of the founders' departures, the same amount would

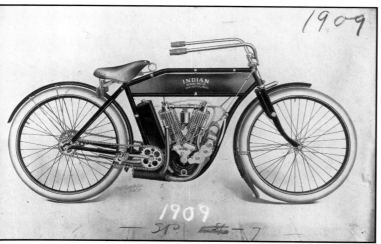

**New loop frame, 1909**
The big news for 1909 was the new loop frame, shown here with the 60.32ci, 989cc twin.
*Hill/Bentley*

purchase a new Ford Model T automobile. Simply put, in terms of today's dollars, peak sales years earned Indian the buying power of $40 million to $50 million annually.

When the new loop-frame look came on the scene in 1909, front suspension was by cartridge spring, rear wheels were unsuspended, all Indians were single-speeders, and single-cylinder motors accounted for most of the sales. At the end of the F-head era, the long-running leaf-spring front fork was in place, most Indians were equipped with rear springs, most were two- or three-speeders, and more than 90 percent were twins. Indian's innovations during these years included America's first footboards and first kickstarter, and the world's first electric starter.

In the sporting realm, board tracks of 1/4- to 1/3-mile lengths—the fabled motordromes—skyrocketed to success between 1909 and 1911. Indian riders dominated the motordromes and to keep the make on top, Hedstrom designed the eight-valve twins that made their debut in 1911; however, between 1912 and 1915 the motordromes fell from favor as suddenly as they had ascended, due to a number of fatal accidents and the fact that the public's curiosity had been satisfied.

Greater glory came to the Wigwam, as the factory was affectionately known, from Indian's 1-2-3 finish at the 1911 Isle of Man road races, and from subsequent record-setting by the star rider

Jake De Rosier. At the end of 1911, Indian riders owned every one of the American records for speed and distance. The Indian and the English Matchless alternated officially as the world's fastest motorcycles, with Indian on top in 1909 at 85mph, and from 1914 throughout the F-head years at 93mph.

After all this glory, Harley-Davidson won America's most prestigious race, the Dodge City 300 of 1915. Harleys also began to win a number of local-interest races. The Harley-Davidson factory-sponsored riders ran at ever-increasing speeds, and put Indian on notice that the Wigwam could no longer assume racing success just by showing up at the starting line.

Another blow to Indian fortunes was the retirement of cofounder and chief engineer Oscar Hedstrom. By 1915, there were increasing rumors of then-president George Hendee's possible retirement as well.

Automobiles were defining the world of transportation in this second decade of the twentieth century. The first drive-in gas station in the United States opened in Pittsburgh, Pennsylvania, in 1913. Prior to that, most motorists purchased their fuel at hardware stores or drug stores. In 1914, the first traffic light in the United States was operated in Cleveland, Ohio. These changes were caused by growing numbers of cars, not motorcycles.

But the biggest change was the motorcycle industry's redefinition of the motorcycle: What was once conceived as a transportation vehicle now was marketed as a sport vehicle. In 1915, Indian sales fell for the second consecutive year. Meanwhile, the American automobile industry grew by 69 percent, with more than 895,000 cars and 74,000 trucks and buses leaving the factories. The Model T Ford was the single largest factor in this fundamental change. Ford started its first moving assembly line in January of 1914; production kept going up and Ford prices kept going

down. No motorcycle factories anywhere in the world could find the new investment money needed to escape the late-nineteenth-century production methods in which their own factories operated.

Realizing that motorcycles would never rival cars in the mass-transportation market, Indian's management placed more and more emphasis on large, expensive motorcycles in the hope of capturing a larger share of the shrinking motorcycle market. Meanwhile, Harley-Davidson had grown explosively from a backyard operation to a serious challenger in the salesrooms and on the racetracks. By 1915, Indian no longer dominated the American motorcycle market. The make remained, however, the most famous of American motorcycles. Indian dealers still had the best stores and still sold more motorcycles than their competitors. The years of the F-head mainstream, then, were years of both glory and success mixed with a leveling off of expectations concerning motorcycling's future.

**Optional belt drive, 1909**
Belt drive was optional on most of the 1909 loop-frame models, this one a 60.32ci twin. *Hill/Bentley*

**Diamond frame holdovers, 1909**
When Indian introduced the new loop frame in the 1909 lineup, the company continued to offer diamond-frame models in order to use up old stock. This is the 1909 38.6ci, 633cc 5hp twin. This example was fitted with the optional three regular-size dry-cell batteries instead of the special three-cell Indian battery. *Hill/Bentley*

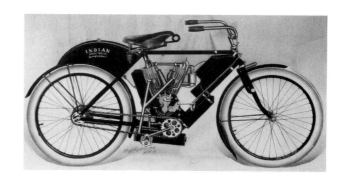

**Arthur Chapple, Daytona Beach, 1909**
Arthur Chapple, expatriate Englishman and Captain of the New York Motorcycle Club, posed for the camera at the April Daytona Beach race meet. Racer features include short exhaust pipes and rearward pipe on the front cylinder. Chapple set ten- and twenty-mile amateur records averaging about 67mph and 69mph respectively. Walter Goerke set a one-kilometer amateur record and a sixty-nine-mile amateur record, averaging about 80mph and 71mph respectively. Goerke's longer record bettered the English hour record of about 68 2/3 miles. Teammate Stubbs set a one-mile amateur record averaging almost 83mph. Indian dominated American record setting, at paces higher than official world's records. Production for 1909 was 4,771 machines. *EMAP Archives*

**G. Lee Evans, Brooklands, 1910**
Rider G. Lee Evans, at the Brooklands track in Surrey, England. Brooklands was a pear-shaped three-mile concrete track opened in 1907, and used through the summer of 1939. Brooklands' existence was a boon to British motorcycle and car designers—as well as to Indian, which consistently won races and set records there in 1910 and 1911. On this day, May 10, 1910, Evans averaged 60mph while finishing second to H. Martin in the two-lap handicap race. On another occasion, Evans rode a 638cc Indian twin to third in the 1910 opening day One Hour Race. He finished behind 638cc Indian riders C. E. Bennett and W. O. Bentley, the man who would establish the legendary automobile line. The following year, Indian dominated Brooklands racing. *EMAP Archives*

**Arthur J. Moorehouse, 1910**
Arthur J. Moorehouse, photographed in March 1910, with the 1909 twin he planned to enter in the Isle of Man TT races. The motorcycle was fitted with a front brake because British law required two brakes for road use. *EMAP Archives.*

**Jake De Rosier, 1911**
Although this photo was taken in 1911, the motorcycle is a 1909 model. On the machine is Indian factory rider Jake De Rosier, who was in England to participate in the Isle of Man TT races, some match races, and some record-setting bouts. From *Motorcycle Illustrated* June 15, 1911, came the following: "Jake De Rosier has arrived in London. The fact has been duly chronicled in the British prints, despite Coronation activities.... Jake barely had time to fill his lungs with the moist ozone of London before a delegation of sporting riders and motorcycle fans fired broadside after broadside of racing queries at him.... Did he expect to win the Tourist Trophy? Did he? Well, rawther." *EMAP Archives.*

**Police Riders, Cincinnati, 1910**
Two Cincinnati policemen show off a 1910 60.92ci, 998cc, with the new leaf spring fork, abbreviated front fender, and new front cylinder exhaust port. Other 1910 improvements included a motor-driven oil pump, four cylinder-hold-down studs on some models, and a two-speed transmission on some models. Police business was an Indian strength from the beginning to the end. New York City helped get Indian police business started by placing their first order in 1903. *EMAP Archives*

**One-speed single, 1911**
The 1911 model 19.30ci, 316cc one-speed single with one of the two styles of long Rough Rider handlegrips, a feature common to all 1911 models. All models for that year also had the new rear stand. Only two finishes were offered in 1911, standard royal blue and optional Indian red. Small parts were in bright nickel, as always. *Hill/Bentley*

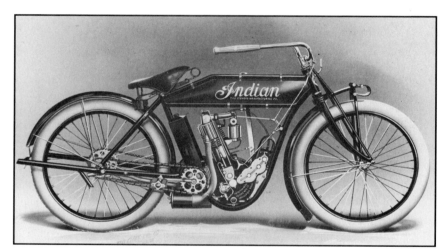

**Regular 7hp Twin Cylinder, 1911**
The Regular 7hp Twin Cylinder single-speed machine had a new bore and stroke combination that increased displacement from 60.32ci to 60.92ci, 998cc. This example has the spark plugs installed in the optional manner, horizontally mounted in the valve pocket. The 1911 motors were substantially redesigned and included new flywheels, crankshafts, and connecting rods. *Hill/Bentley*

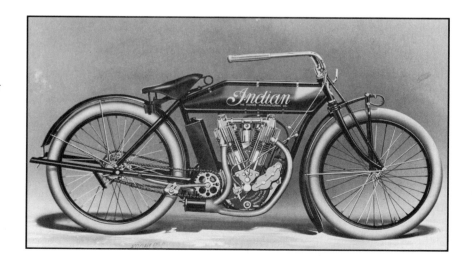

**Charles B. Franklin, Isle of Man TT, 1911**
Ready for the 1911 Isle of Man TT, already the world's premier road race, was Irishman Charles B. Franklin. The Indian team consisted of De Rosier, Franklin, Moorehouse, and Oliver C. Godfrey. Their machines were production models sleeved down to 35.7ci (585cc) to comply with TT rules. The Indian two-speed counter-shaft gearbox and all-chain drive were important advantages over single-speed and belt-drive opposition because for the first time, the TT was to be contested over the mountain route. Franklin was later to become chief engineer at Indian. *EMAP archives*

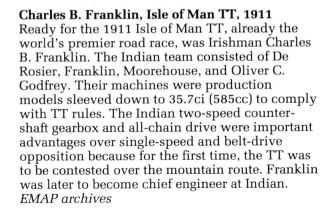

**Isle of Man TT, Pre-World War I era**
Some idea of the early TT course is seen in this 1909 photo of the road to Peel. Baxter on a Rex leads Indian-mounted Lee Evans. This was the first running of the 37-mile mountain circuit that included a 1,350-foot climb from sea level over the zenith of Snaefell Summit. Prior to the 1911 TT there had been stubborn opposition in Britain to the use of "variable gears." The 1911 TT established this feature as a necessity. *EMAP archives*

**Oliver C. Godfrey wins the TT, 1911**
Godfrey is flagged home on his Indian. There was no other rider in sight, partly because the TT featured staggered starting. Godfrey was the TT winner, while Indian riders Franklin and Moorehouse finished second and third. The well-known Jake De Rosier, victim of several crashes in the practice rounds, nevertheless led the first lap and then crashed on the third lap, finishing a dazed twelfth. England's popular Charlie Collier, cofounder with brother Harry of the Matchless marque, would have finished second if he hadn't been disqualified for taking on fuel at an unauthorized point. The TT win boosted British Indian sales, which were already high. *EMAP archives*

**Jake De Rosier, England, 1911**
DeRosier with the motorcycle he used in a series of three Brooklands match races against Matchless rider/builder Charles Collier. In the first two-lap race, De Rosier won by less than one length. In the second race, a five-lapper, De Rosier's Indian suffered a blowout. The third and deciding ten-lap race, a 27-miler, was marred when Collier's Matchless had a plug wire come loose. The results were widely debated, but De Rosier proved his mettle by later setting Brooklands records for the mile and the kilometer at more than 88mph. *A. F. Van Order via Bob Smith*

**Los Angeles Stadium motordrome, 1912**
From Stephen Wright's *American Racer*, we learn: This was a "three-lap" track, measuring 1/3 mile in circumference. The wooden planking was left in rough cut finish, to provide better traction for the 2in tires. Speeds steadily increased and 90mph laps became common. Crowds of 10,000 were typical. *Bob Smith*

**4hp 30.50, 1912**
The 4hp 30.50, a belt-drive single, in its second year of production. Indian described conventional belt slippage arrangements as "cheap and slip-shod." Indian's answer was a conventional clutch incorporated in the drive pulley. *Hill/Bentley*

**Tex Richards, 1912**
For American board tracks, the dominant machine through the spring of 1911 was the Indian F-head. The rider here was Tex Richards. Note the steep banking of the track; earlier tracks were less steeply banked, but by 1912, 60-degree banking was standard. The steep banking threatened riders with becoming airborne should they lose control in the turns. *Dave Kinnie collection, donated by Bud Cox*

**Charles Balke and big-base eight-valve twin, 1912**
Shortly after Indian's 1-2-3 dominance of the 1911 Isle of Man TT, Indian unveiled about six or so impressive eight-valve twins that were used to continue the marque's dominance of American board track racing. This is Charles "Fearless" Balke aboard a big-base eight-valve at the Playa Del Rey (Los Angeles area) 1-mile board track. Balke and Playa Del Rey were credited with the first officially timed 100mph run in December 1912. However, the first official "ton up" machine was an Excelsior. *Stephen Wright*

**Eddie Hasha and big-base eight-valve twin, 1912**
In 1912, motordrome star Eddie Hasha won races at speeds averaging more than 90mph over 1/4- and 1/3-mile steeply banked wooden tracks! Board track speeds consistently exceeded the official motorcycle world record, 91.23mph. The United States did a poor job of handling its international racing politics. In September 1912, the unfortunate Hasha, another racer, and six spectators were killed in the deadliest motorcycle racing accident in American history. The motordromes declined rapidly afterward. *EMAP archives*

**British soldier and Indian twin, 1912**
A British soldier works on his 1912 twin. The front exhaust pipe had reverted to the 1909 and earlier style, exiting downward. *EMAP archives*

**Indian twin with wicker sidecar, 1912**
What the British called a colonial sidecar outfit, this example featuring a fancy wicker body. *Ian Campbell*

**Customizing, 1913**
From the very first days of motorcycling, riders have sought to imbue their machines with unique qualities by adding features or taking off equipment. This Englishman has gone the "full dress" route, and appears to have added a two-speed rear hub to his original one-speed machine. *EMAP archives*

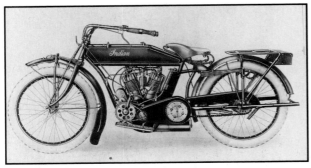

**First kickstarter, 1913**
The hallmark feature of the 1913 line was the new swinging-arm rear suspension, dubbed the Cradle Spring Frame. This is the 60.92ci, 998.33cc TT twin, which featured Indian's first kickstarter, improved rear brake, and knockout front and rear axles. Ninety percent of all 1913 Indians were twins. *Bob Finn*

**Indian Side Car, 1914**
Sidecars made their first sales catalog appearance in 1914. Within a year, sidecar sales exceeded 3,000 annually. *George and Milli Yarocki*

**Postman, 1913**
Motorcycles were popular with rural mail carriers. Indian and other American manufacturers showed exhibits at postal conventions. The US Postal Service banned motorcycles in the late teens, however, due to accidents. *EMAP archives*

# OSCAR HEDSTROM RETIRES

Oscar Hedstrom, long a prime factor in the development of Indian motorcycles as vice-president of the Hendee Manufacturing Co., announces his retirement from active participation in the company's affairs, and states that his only plans for the present concern a long recreation trip on which he has had his mind set for some time. Mr. Hedstrom's retirement becomes effective March 1.

*From* Motorcycle Illustrated, *March 6, 1913*

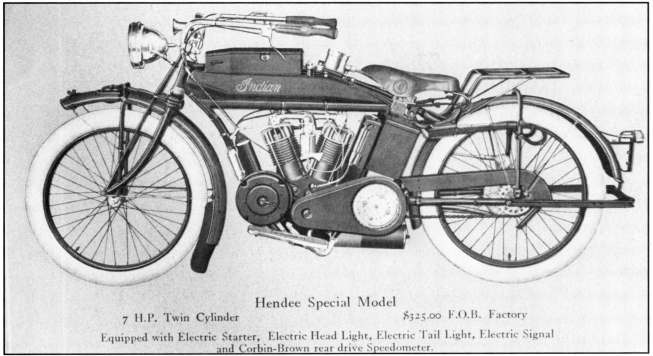

Hendee Special Model

7 H.P. Twin Cylinder                    $325.00 F.O.B. Factory

Equipped with Electric Starter, Electric Head Light, Electric Tail Light, Electric Signal
and Corbin-Brown rear drive Speedometer.

**Hendee Special, 1914**
The Hendee Special introduced electric starting to the motorcycle world. Two batteries were provided, but no generator, and owners had to charge the batteries overnight. Thus, the self-starter feature was both inconvenient and unreliable. *George and Milli Yarocki*

**Pancho Villa and Hendee Special, 1914**
Mexican revolutionary leader Pancho Villa tries out a 1914 Hendee Special. *EMAP archives*

**End of an era, 1915**
The 1915 F-heads marked the end of their era. This machine, owned and restored by the late Dewey Bonkrud, shows the three-speed transmission that was new for 1915.

**Indian factory, 1914**

This photo was taken about 1935, but is representative of the final form of the famous Indian factory, as it appeared in late 1914. Known worldwide as the Wigwam, the factory was located at the intersection of State Street (on the left) and Wilbraham Road (on the right). As the world's largest motorcycle factory, the Wigwam was designed to produce 60,000 motorcycles annually on a two- and three-shift basis. However, production never rose above the 1913 high of 32,000 units. Company grounds included an area of over 1 million square feet (19 acres), 7 miles of walkways connecting the thirty-five departments, and $1 million worth of machinery (more than $50 million in today's dollars). *Bob Finn*

**Brooklands record, 1914.**

At Brooklands, in June 1914, are timekeeper A. V. Ebblewhite in the sidecar, Indian distributor Billy Wells standing in the center with cap, Charles B. Franklin on the eight-valve twin, and Oliver C. Godfrey standing next to Franklin. During the year at Brooklands, Godfrey rode an eight-valve to a new British record of 93.48mph, well below American board track speeds due to Brooklands' rough concrete surface. On this occasion, Franklin set a 10-mile record of 77.95mph. *EMAP archives*

**Generator electrics, 1915**
All 1915 Indians could be furnished with optional electric lighting, as shown on this 60.92ci, 998.33cc Big Twin. New for 1915 was the provision of a generator. The 1915 frames were made of chrome-vanadium steel. *Bob Finn*

**The little twin, 1915**
Some motorcycle journalists had been clamoring for a smaller twin, so for the 1915 season Indian introduced the Little Twin, a 41.58ci, 681.32cc machine. Demand didn't live up to expectations, so the model lasted only one year on the American market. *EMAP archives*

**Gun car, 1915**
This machine-gun-equipped
twin was marketed by Indian to
the British army. Whether any
were purchased is unknown.
*EMAP archives*

**Chicago board track, circa 1915**
As the short motordromes faded
from popularity in the early
teens, board tracks of 1-mile or
more circumference gained in
favor. They were built primarily
for automobile racing. *Geoff
Hockley*

**Model D-1 Speedway, 1915**
"Speedway" was the American
term for a long dirt track,
generally either a 1/2-mile or
1-mile circuit. *George and Milli
Yarocki*

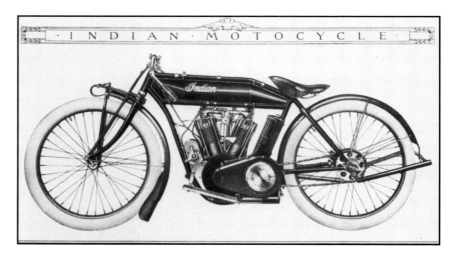

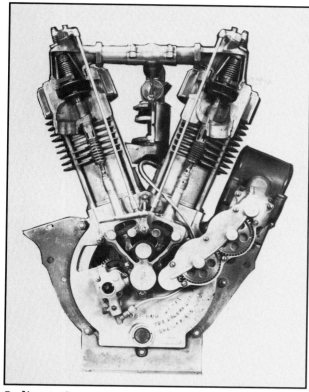

**Indian twin, 1915**
An example of the Hedstrom-designed F-head,
or inlet-over-exhaust (IOE), motor that powered
Indian through its greatest days. *Bob Finn*

# EARL BECOMES INDIAN MANAGER
*Former Assistant Manager
Succeeds Mr. Hendee
as the
Active Head of the
Company*

SPRINGFIELD, MASS.—Announcement has
just been made by the Hendee Manufacturing Company that Mr. George Hendee has
resigned as general manager of the company, these duties having been assumed by
Mr. Clarence A. Earl who acted in the
capacity of assistant manager the past
twelve months....

*From* Motorcycle Illustrated, *April 29, 1915*

# THE VELVET HAMMER
*Breezy Comments in Rhyme....*

When one wheel of the bike was low
and t'other one was high, and accidents
were similar to falling from the sky, George
Hendee was the champion who made the
tallest speed by pushing on the pedals of the
steel and rubber steed, without the easy
comfort that the modern lad admires,
derived from gentle breezes cushioning
inflated tires.

Though nature had provided him with
tough and wiry pegs, he often felt that
weariness was creeping up his legs, and as
his wheel devoured the miles and gobbled
up the hours, he found that world-wide
champions have limits to their powers; and
he evolved the happy plan within his merry
bean to have the hard and heavy work performed by gasoline.

And now a million folks or more are
burning up the pike, and riding George's little dream, the Indian motobike; they pass
you on the boulevards, a red and rapid
streak, bestowing heat and fervor on the lan-
guage that you speak; unlike the ancient
Cherokees, they do not lift your skelp, but
they extort from out your chest a brief and
nervous yelp.

So large have been his profits from the
demon fast and red that George has found
he could afford to slack his speed and wed.
So while he spends his honeymoon on far
Pacific coast, you'll kindly stand upon your
feet and join us in a toast: "Long live his
benzine trotting horse; may business never
balk, and leave its owner far from home, to
push it and to walk!"

*—From* The Springfield (Mass.) Union

# Chapter 3

# 1916–1919

## *The Powerplus Interlude*

For the 1916 season, Indian startled the motorcycling world by killing off the historic Hedstrom series of F-head twins and singles. The new lineup had all valves on the side. This brought the advantages of cleaner and quieter operation, as well as more power, resulting in the Powerplus designation.

**The Wigwam, 1919**
Scenes from the Wigwam, as published in *Motorcycling and Bicycling* in May 1919.

The Powerplus series got a rousing send off in late 1915 when noted long-distance hauler Erwin G. "Cannonball" Baker, already the transcontinental record-holder aboard an F-head Indian, used a preproduction Powerplus to set a new Canada-to-Mexico Three Flag record.

Although the Powerplus models were an engineering success, the development cost was substantial and sales of 22,000 motorcycles yielded a profit of only $208,000. This was less than half the profit for the previous year for about the same production level. Moreover, conventional accounting practices meant these Powerplus development costs would continue to be amortized over the next several years.

Indian president George Hendee retired in July 1916, and pursued the leisure life on his Connecticut farm. He was succeeded by John F. Alvord of New York City.

In early 1917, America entered World War I. Indian's new management saw the war as a golden opportunity and negotiated a large contract for military motorcycles for the United States Army.

The perception has been that the company lost considerable money by selling motorcycles to the Army. Financially, Indian did well in the military motorcycle business. Profits for the years 1917, 1918, and 1919 were $540,000, $733,000, and $937,000, respectively. Profits for 1919 were the second largest in company history, although inflation undoubtedly diluted the meaning. But profits aside, the Indian-Army contract was indeed bad business, as a magazine headline made clear: "Indian Deliveries Contingent On Needs Of Government." In addition to the loss of many potential riders who were now serving in the military, Indian dealers also were faced with the unavailability of motorcycles due to the company's military production.

Harley-Davidson, which didn't make such a big commitment to military production, made inroads into Indian civilian sales from 1917 through 1919. At the time, Indian practiced what today's business schools call "pull demand," where Indian's reputation would "pull" customers through Indian dealer doorways. The demand for Indian motorcycles was so strong for so many years that the Hendee Manufacturing Company dictated conditions to its dealers. These conditions were many, and included not only wholesale prices, but credit arrangements and minimum-order quantities.

The destiny and success of both Indian and The Harley-Davidson Motor Company were intertwined. At this stage, Harley-Davidson, as the new up-and-coming manufacturer, was far more eager to please current and potential dealers in order to strengthen its dealer network. Selfish interest aside—and the old Harley-Davidson company could be ruthless—Indian's Milwaukee rival developed what business schools call "push demand." Push demand means that a company doesn't assume success, but instead relies on strong advertising and promotion, sales incentives to its dealers, price cutting, and anything else it can think of to promote its product. Promotion to Harley-Davidson meant selling to dealers as customers, not just selling to riders.

To its long-run detriment, Indian was too successful too soon, which nourished in Harley-Davidson the notion that the real customers were dealers, not riders. This is still a sound notion.

**Powerplus Model F, 1916**
The biggest news for 1916 was the new line of Powerplus models that replaced the historic Hedstrom F-head range. The impetus for the new motors was cost savings, but the new side-valve motors were also more powerful, cleaner, and quieter. The Powerplus range was the brainchild of Charles Gustafson, Sr., who had earlier worked for the Reading Standard motorcycle company, builders of America's first side-valve motorcycles. This is the basic 1916 big twin, the Model F with spring frame. No Powerplus singles were included in the 1916 catalogs. *George Hays*

But the Hendee Manufacturing Company for too long thought its Indian dealers did little more than accept sales commissions on sales that were guaranteed by the Indian reputation. Thus, by the end of 1919 the stage was set for an all-out sales war between Indian and Harley-Davidson.

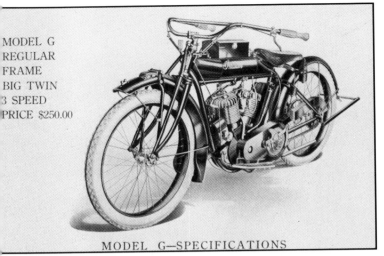

MODEL G
REGULAR
FRAME
BIG TWIN
3 SPEED
PRICE $250.00

MODEL G—SPECIFICATIONS

**Powerplus Model G, 1916**
For 1916, buyers could opt for less-expensive
rigid-frame big twins. Extra seat springs were
installed on rigid-frame models.

**Featherweight two-stroke, 1916**
Built along English lines, the 1916 Featherweight
single lasted only one year on the American
market. The motor featured a piston with a large
deflector to help separate the inlet and exhaust
charges; this was common two-stroke practice
until the late 1930s. Restoration by Paul Pearce.

NEW INDIAN POWERPLUS MOTOR IN SECTION

**Powerplus, 1916**
Powerplus cylinders and heads were cast in
one piece, access to the valves being provided by
hexagonal valve caps. The inlet and exhaust
valves were the same size, which Indian claimed
as an advantage because the rider was obliged
to take along only one spare valve. As in the
F-heads, an external oil line was routed to the
base of the front cylinder to compensate for the
less-effective flywheel oil sling up front. Another
F-head carryover was the use of a single camshaft
to operate all valves. The Powerplus magneto
platform was cast into the crankcase, instead of
relying on mounting plates.

**Small-base eight-valve twin, 1916**
About 1916, a new series of eight-valve twins and four-valve singles made its debut. The new engines used conventional F-head crankcases and eventually were referred to as small-base models, their predecessors being called big-base models to distinguish the two types. *Sam Hotton*

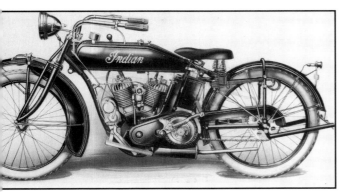

**Powerplus, 1917**
The 1917 models were the last with bell crank control linkages and the first with split gas tanks that hid the top frame tube. The new tanks were not only more stylish, but were also cheaper to build than the earlier tanks. Mandatory black wheel rims and hubs replaced the former nickel-plated items. *Hill/Bentley*

**Small-base eight-valve twins, 1916**
A couple of small-base eight-valve twins, seen in a racing pit typical for the era. *Kinnie/Cox*

**Model O Light Twin, 1917**
With the 1916 Featherweight two-stroke having proved a mistake, Indian decided to replace it with a four-stroke horizontally opposed twin called the Model O Light Twin. It was smooth running and quiet, but the American motorcycle market was already moving away from a transportation emphasis to a sport emphasis. Riders of other brands termed the new Indian lightweight the Model Nothing. Restoration by Paul Pearce.

**Model O Light Twin, 1917**
This Light Twin was hitchhiking by air, probably more of a publicity stunt than an actual military practice. *Hill/Bentley*

**Light Twin, 1918**
The 1918 Light Twin had a new leaf spring fork. Another new feature was the "trolley car" gearshift lever, which imparted a rotary motion to the vertical rod. *Hill/Bentley*

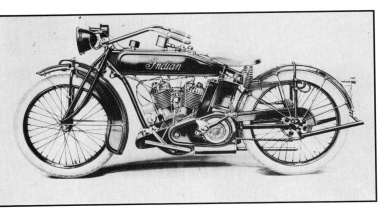

**Powerplus, 1918**
Detail changes continued on the Powerplus F-heads, including wire controls, a new saddle mounting, new horn, and new headlight. A new electrical setup featured a separate magneto and generator instead of the combined unit used in 1917. The low mounting of the Splitdorf generator drew criticism from dealers and riders. *Hill/Bentley*

**Powerplus, circa 1918**
Rider's view of a Powerplus. Restoration by Marv Baker.

*Right*
**Indian factory race team, 1919**
The Indian factory team, either getting a great jump on the field in the rolling start, or, more likely, taking a warmup lap at Marion, Indiana. Over the Labor Day weekend, a 200-mile national championship road race was conducted in 1919 and 1920 on rural roads. Harley-Davidson won both the 1919 and 1920 Marion 200s, despite full factory team efforts of Indian and Excelsior. Coupled with Harley's Dodge City wins of 1915, 1916, 1920, and 1921, Indian prestige was greatly damaged. *Harley-Davidson*

# Indian Deliveries Contingent on Needs of Government

*There Will Be Indian Motorcycles, Sidecars and Delivery Cars
for Civilian Buyers, But How Many and When Depends Entirely
Upon the Requirements of Our Fighting Forces and Those of Our
Allies Whose Orders Will Be Filled First*
Standardized by the Tests of Battlefield
*No Basic Changes in Indian Construction for 1919—*
*Constantly Changing Conditions in Material and Labor*
*Supply Compel Announcement That Prices Are Subject to Change without Notice and*
*Orders Subject to Price at Time of Delivery*

SPRINGFIELD, Mass., September 18—

The Indian motorcycle has been drafted for the duration of the war. Until Germany flies the white flag of unconditional surrender, every machine, every muscle and every brain in the Hendee organization is "with the colors."

"Uncle Same comes first." These four words are the text of the Indian announcement for the season of 1919, or so much of it as shall have elapsed between now and the allied victory which General March has said will be next summer.

**Civilians Come Second**

This does not mean that there will be no new Indians for civilian riders until the war is over, but it does mean that civilian riders must be content and glad to get whatever may be left for them after the Government orders have been filled.

**Delivery is Uncertain**

There will be Indian Powerplus twins, Indian opposed motor light twins, Indian sidecars and Indian parcel cars for civilian buyers next season, but when and how many will depend entirely upon the ability of the Hendee Mfg. Company to get the material and turn out the machines in greater numbers than the fighting forces call for them.

**Early orders Advisable**

Because of this uncertainty dealers are advised to place their orders at once. This does not mean that the dealers who send in their specifications now are promised deliveries this fall or at any other specified time, but it does mean that if the Government gives an opportunity, to supply a portion of the civilian needs, as it is hoped will be the case, the dealers whose orders are on record will be the ones to get the machines.

From *Motorcycle and Bicycle Illustrated*, September 19, 1918

**"Cannonball" Baker and Powerplus, 1919**
Trying for another transcontinental record in June 1919, Erwin G. "Cannonball" Baker was stopped by rain and mud when three-fourths of the way across, in New Mexico. Here, he's seen earlier on the east-west run, greeted in Philadelphia by fans.
*Motorcycle and Bicycle Illustrated*

*Left*
**Dave Kinnie and Roy Artley, circa 1919**
Goodyear sales representative Dave Kinnie poses with Indian factory rider Roy Artley at one of the Marion road races. Powerplus motors had become the backbone of Indian racing.
*Kinnie/Cox*

**"Cannonball" Baker, circa 1920**
"Cannonball" Baker was a large man with "hands like hams," recalled his friend and competitor Maldwyn Jones. Although Baker was noted for long rides with little sleep, Jones related that "Bake" fell asleep easily in the midst of social conversation that didn't interest him. *Kinnie/Cox*

# Cannonball Baker

Of all those whose glory came from long-distance record setting, none surpassed Erwin G. "Cannonball" Baker of Indianapolis, Indiana. "Bake," as he was called by his closest friends, was tall and big boned. His hands were like hams, one of them said.

Baker tried his hand at flat track racing and despite his large physique he had his share of wins. His first big win was the Ten Mile National Championship of 1909, a dirt track race conducted on the sight of the forthcoming Indianapolis Motor Speedway two years before the first Indianapolis 500 car race. In 1911, Baker won the July the Fourth "President's Race" at Indianapolis, and afterwards received the personal congratulations of President William Howard Taft. To date, Baker is the only motorcycle racer to be afforded this honor.

Baker caught the attention of Indian president George Hendee, who hired Baker to conduct a goodwill tour of Cuba, Jamaica, and Panama in order to boost sales in the tropics. Baker responded with a 14,000 miles of riding. This was Baker's first of many Indian assignments. For the next several years he would continue to live up to unwritten deals made over the handshakes of George Hendee and subsequent Indian negotiators.

Despite his strong identification with Indian motorcycles and the transcontinental record, Baker set only one transcontinental record on an Indian. That came in May 1914, when Cannonball rode from San Diego to New York City in 11 days, 12 hours, and 10 minutes. He chopped nine days off the previous record. The record ride took him over four mountain ranges, 1,027 miles of desert, 232 miles of prairie mud, and sixty-four bone jarring miles of railroad track. His trail went as low as 200 feet below sea level and as high as 10,000 feet in mountain passes.

Later in 1914, Baker won the 537-mile Borderline Derby race on an Indian, streaking from El Paso to Phoenix in 15 hours and 52 minutes. A New York City newspaper man called Baker a "cannonball," and the nickname stuck.

His next glory came in August 1915, from the first of many "Three Flag" runs conducted along the 1,655.5 miles separating the Canadian and Mexican borders. Cannonball did the honors in 3 days, 9 hours, and 15 minutes. His mount was a new Powerplus side-valve, which had not yet publicly debuted in the Indian lineup.

In 1916, Baker conducted an Australian tour for Hendee. On a course near Mortlake, Australia, he set a 24-hour record of 1,018 3/4 miles despite dealing with large flocks of rabbits, frightened king-sized parakeets, and torrential rain. After completing the run, his dried leather suit had become so stiff that it had to be cut away from his body.

In 1917, at the Cincinnati Speedway Cannonball set a new 24-hour record of 1,534 3/4 miles over the board track, using an Indian Powerplus. Then in 1919, he was one of seven survivors out of an entry list of thirty who finished the San Francisco Motorcycle Club endurance run. The course consisted of two round-trips between San Francisco and Santa Cruz, California, totaling 580.4 miles, and included rain, hail, snow, and a landslide. Baker finished third overall.

The transcontinental record had since been taken over by Alan Bedell, who rode a four-cylinder Henderson. Baker accepted another handshake deal with Indian in 1919, but his transcontinental attempt was spoiled by bad weather. Likewise, in 1921 Baker and passenger Erle Armstrong were unsuccessful in an attempt on the transcontinental sidecar record.

Thereafter, Baker was lured away from Indian by the makers of the four-cylinder Ace, for whom he set another transcontinental record in 1922. "Cannonball Baker" was now a household name in America, so Baker enjoyed temporary employment by several automobile companies. He continued to criss-cross the continent in search of new records. Also in 1922, he rode a lightweight Neracar two-stroke motorcycle from coast to coast to demonstrate its reliability, averaging 20mph across the continent.

Baker's last transcontinental motorcycle outing was in 1941. This run was made to test a rotary-valve single-cylinder engine, which he is credited to have assisted in design.

*Chapter 4*

# 1920–1929

## *Great Motorcycles, Bad Business*

The mid-size Indian Scout 37ci, 600cc V-twin was a sensation when introduced in the line-up of 1920 models. The side-valve Scout combined advanced engineering with surprising power and unbeatable reliability, offering riders the best of both worlds—easy handling plus enough power to ride as fast as permitted by most roads of 1920. As well as being a good seller, the new middleweight served as an entry-level

**Sidecar racing, circa 1920**
Sidecar racing was so popular in the early 1920s that the sidecar final was the feature event at some race meets. The middle outfit in front is a conventional sidecar rig, but the left and right outfits feature a banking Flexi sidecar. The Flexi rigs were practically unbeatable in dirt-track racing. *Kinnie/Cox*

model that brought new riders into the game, riders who were put off by big twins.

For the 1922 season, Indian brought out the 61ci, 1000cc Chief, which was advertised as "a big Scout." Since many American riders still believed bigger was better, the 1923 season saw the introduction of the 74ci, 1200cc Big Chief. The Big Chief immediately took over the role of sales leader.

The Scout backed up its initial rave reviews with continuous good results in the hands of riders everywhere. Two Scout records in 1923 startled the motorcycle world as rider Paul Remaly set new Canada-to-Mexico and transcontinental records.

The next Indian model to make its debut in 1925 was the Prince 21ci, 350cc side-valve single; a year later it came in an overhead-valve version. Harley-Davidson also launched its 350cc side-valve model in 1925 and followed up with an overhead-valve derivative. Both companies were impressed with British and European sales of similar models: Harley-Davidson records reveal that their main sales targets were Europe, Australia, and New Zealand; despite no similar Indian records, the company probably had the same strategy. In any case, sales of the Prince single were disappointing, perhaps because there just wasn't a big enough market for both Indian and Harley-Davidson.

During the 1927 season, Indian brought out probably the best engine it ever built, the 45ci, 750cc V-twin that served out its life as the muscle of the famous Model 101 Scout (which was not yet introduced). The new "Forty-five" was a happy combination of bore, stroke, and other factors, and the motor seemed to work better than it should have. Placed in the standard Scout frame, the new model was designated as the Police Special, as cop bikes in those days had a reputation for speed.

Equally noteworthy in 1927 was Indian's purchase of the manufacturing rights and production tooling for the four-cylinder Ace motorcycle. Indian advertising proudly referred to its "full line" of singles, twins, and fours. Within months the green Ace gave way to the red Indian Ace, then to the Indian Four, the latter with traditional Indian leaf-spring forks.

In 1928, a midseason announcement proclaimed the new Model 101 Scout, which was achieved by lengthening and lowering the standard Scout. Paralleling the happy combination of factors that made the 45ci motor just right, the new 101 frame combined stability and agility in a way that no design before or since has equaled.

Despite an aggressive engineering program, however, Indian sales in the twenties slipped ever further behind those of Harley-Davidson, whose bikes had become big sellers in Australia and New Zealand. Harley-Davidson, by virtue of repeated wins in the more glamorous long-distance races, had become *the* high-performance American motorcycle. For instance, in 1920 Indian won fourteen national championship races at distances of from 1 to 50 miles, with total winning mileage of 200 miles, whereas Harley-Davidson won 511 miles of racing spread over only three races.

More fundamental to Indian's slipping position was its continual dabbling in things nonmotorcycle. Nonmotorcycle production items included automobile shock absorbers, automobile ventilators, and outboard motors, all of which proved unprofitable. Central to these excursions was the makeup of Indian's controlling management group, whose members were neither motorcycle enthusiasts nor professional manufacturers. Instead, they were financiers whose view of the company was that of a production facility and that anything that was built there could be sold. They didn't understand that among Indian's most valuable assets were its marketing know-how and its person-to-person contacts in the highly specialized motorcycle field. To worsen matters, a few genuine crooks took over the management in the late twenties and milked the company's treasury.

By the end of the roaring twenties, Indian was perilously close to shutting down.

**Scout, 1920**
The sensation of Indian's 1920 line was the Scout, which featured a semi-unit-construction powerplant with the transmission bolted to the back of the engine. Connecting the two was an indestructible helical gear primary drive, enclosed in a cast-aluminum cover, and running in an oil bath. This example is configured with the Harley-Davidson-style (meaning backward!) clutch pedal action. Indians were normally configured with the clutch rod on top of the clutch center, which resulted in a toe-down action to disengage the clutch. *Hill/Bentley*

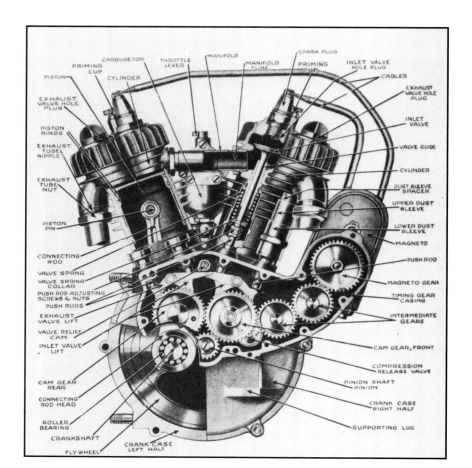

**Scout, 1920**
The Scout 37ci (nominal), 600cc motor differed from the earlier Powerplus big twin by using two camshafts instead of one. These motors proved to be nearly indestructible. Seven years later, the displacement would be enlarged 25 percent to 45ci (nominal), 750cc with no problems encountered.

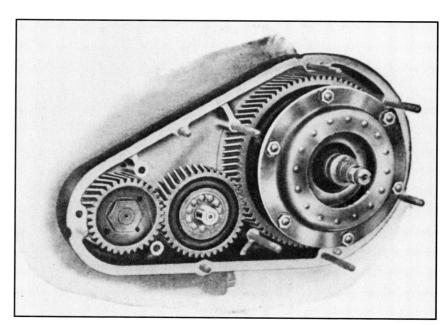

**Scout, 1920**
The Scout primary drive system, a vast improvement over contemporary practice, featured helical gears running in an oil bath cast-aluminum chain case.

**Scout, 1921**
For 1921, the Scout received a new luggage rack with extra braces, and a new sidestand of tubular cross section. *Hill/Bentley*

**Herbert LeVack and big-base eight-valve twin, 1921**
The rider is Herbert "Bert" LeVack, and if he looks a little solemn, this may be because he already knows that the honor of the first 100mph motorcycle ride in Britain has already gone to Harley-Davidson rider D. H. Davidson (no relation to *the* Davidsons). A day after Davidson motored 100.76mph, LeVack and his circa 1912 Indian upped the British record to 107.5mph. *Hill/Bentley*

**Russell Coes and TT single, 1921**
One of the 1921 Isle of Man TT team machines, held up by team manager Russell Coes, a Canadian. Earlier Indian teams had used twins. The 1921 racing motors were made by converting V-twins to singles. ( I call them half-twins, but they weren't called that in their day.) *EMAP archives*

## Board track, circa 1921

From 1919 through the late 1920s, a number of 1-mile or longer board tracks were frequently used for national championship motorcycle racing. Locations included Beverly Hills, California; Chicago, Illinois; Salem, New Hampshire; Brooklyn, New York; and Altoona, Pennsylvania. From 1919 through 1921, Harley-Davidson generally beat Indian in the longer events, culminating in Harley-Davidson winning *every* 1921 national championship. Harley-Davidson dropped factory racing support in 1922, then gradually got back into the game. Racing glory was then pretty evenly split until Indian won *every* national racing title in both 1928 and 1929. Interest in long board-track racing waned in the late twenties. Increasing maintenance costs, opportunities to sell out to real estate developers, and the economic disaster of the Great Depression combined to kill off these dramatic facilities. *Harley-Davidson*

## Freddie Dixon, Isle of Man TT, 1921

Rider Freddie Dixon at speed in the 1921 TT, on his way to second place on a "half-twin" Indian. Indian teammate Bert LeVack finished third, and Indian won the team prize. This was as close as Indian ever got to repeating their 1911 TT triumph. Who won first place, you ask? Howard R. Davies, on a 350cc AJS, beat all the 500cc jobs home. *EMAP archives*

## Chief, 1922

Big news for 1922 was the Chief, a 60.88ci, 998cc twin inspired by the Scout. The Chief was destined to have one of the longest production runs in the history of motorcycling. Too bad we can't return the photo to the Indian advertising department, as the stamp says! *Hill/Bentley*

**Chief, 1922**
This 1922 Chief is outfitted with a front-fender-mounted license plate, front wheel stand, and dual brakes, to meet British requirements. *EMAP Archives*

*Left*
**Chief and sidecar, 1922**
The Chief was advertised as primarily a sidecar hauler. *Hill/Bentley*

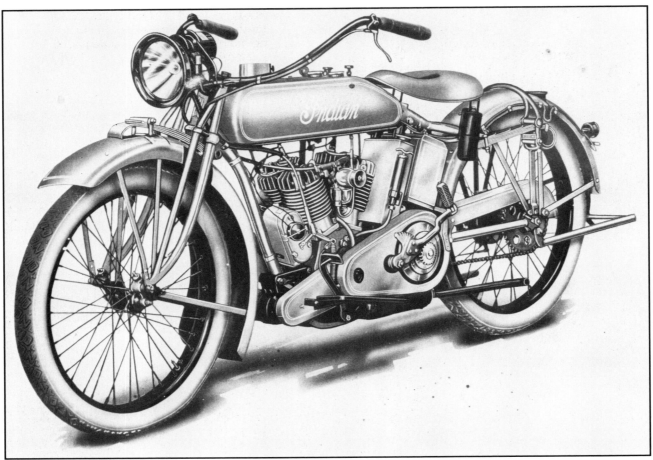

**Standard, 1922**

For 1922, the Powerplus was renamed the Standard to keep from implying the new Chief had less power than the older model. The large crowned or valanced front and rear fenders were new for 1922, as was the rear fender hinge to ease tire changes. A new sidecar frame was designed for the Chief, while the earlier Powerplus sidecar frame remained in production for the Standard models. *Hill/Bentley*

**Powerplus gets a name change, 1922**

When the Chief came out as a 1922 model, the Powerplus twin was renamed the Standard. This Standard shows the enclosed seat springs that came out that year on the Standard and Chief. *Hill/Bentley*

**Freddie Dixon, Belgian Gran Prix, 1923**
Rider Freddie Dixon posed for the camera after winning the important 1923 Belgian Gran Prix for Indian. *EMAP archives*

**Freddie Dixon, Isle of Man TT, 1923**
Dixon's fondness for both Indians and Harley-Davidsons extended to the use of footboards instead of the footpegs favored by other British and continental racers. Dixon rode a Douglas outfit to victory in the Sidecar TT on Wednesday of race week and was favored by many to win Friday's Senior TT on his Indian. However, tire trouble on the third lap cost Dixon several minutes and he finished third, just two and a half minutes behind the winner. *EMAP archives*

## Paul Remaly and record-setting Scout, 1923

Rider Paul Remaly aboard his record-setting 36.4ci, 596cc Scout. Back in 1919, the Motorcycle and Allied Trades Association, or M & ATA, instituted a policy of no longer sanctioning record runs over public roads. That didn't stop Indian, Henderson, and Ace from continuing this colorful tradition. In May 1923, Remaly rode from Tijuana, Mexico, to Blaine, British Columbia, in 46 hours, 58 minutes, breaking a Three Flag record held by Wells Bennett on a 1300cc Henderson Four. In June, Bennett lowered the Three Flag mark to 46 hours, 9 minutes. In July, Remaly fired back with a Scout Three Flag run in 43 hours, 21 minutes, heaping further embarrassment on the Henderson marque, which had advertised that any long-distance record worth having was held by Henderson. In August, Remaly grew tired of the Three Flag game and took aim on the transcontinental record of 6 days, 16 hours, and 13 minutes, another Henderson achievement. Remaly and the little Scout amazed motorcyclists by crossing the continent in 5 days, 17 hours, and 10 minutes, beating the Henderson time by more than 22 hours. Shortly afterward, Indian announced that it would no longer support record runs over public roads, due to its position as a major supplier to police departments. *Hill/Bentley*

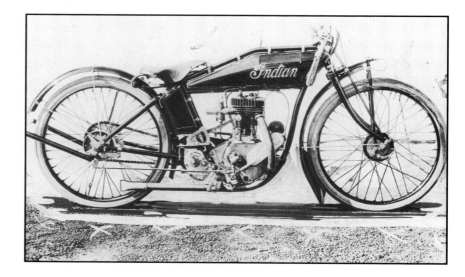

## Dixon's TT racer, 1923

Another look at the 1923 Dixon racer. *EMAP Archives*

**Rollie Free and Ace four, 1923**
Pardon the Ace motorcycle, but its appearance here provides a benchmark for comparison with the later Indian Ace from four and five years later. The real reason for this photo is that it shows the late Roland "Rollie" Free as a young man, at about the time he dedicated his motorcycling life to combatting Harley-Davidson. In the autumn, he went to work for Al Crocker at the Kansas City Indian agency. *Rollie Free*

# Street Racing

In September 1923, young Roland "Rollie" Free competed in the 100-Mile National Championship race at Kansas City. He and his Harley-Davidson were no match for the top stars with factory prepared machines, such as Harley's Jim Davis and Indian's Curly Fredericks. Free felt cheated by the Kansas City Harley dealer, and a quarrel escalated into a lawsuit by the Harley dealer against Free's sponsor. Free dedicated his life to getting revenge against all things Harley.

Rollie called on Kansas City Indian dealer Al Crocker and asked for a job selling Indians, vowing, "I'll work twenty-four hours a day. You give me a fast Indian and I'll fix your town for you." He was hired.

Armed with a new "B" motor Chief, Free agitated the local Harley crowd. "I'd go down by the Harley shop at night when they're all out in front drinking beer out of the growler—the can across the road. And they used to crowd Indian guys into the curbing. When they'd go by, they'd jump on bikes, run up, and crowd'em into the curbing. They were rough! I went down—and I was a little nutty of course—and I said, 'Look, I'm going to ride up and down by here, and if any of you fellas want to do any crowding, come on out.' I said, 'When you pick yourselves up, I'll still be going up and down, 'cause I'll kick front wheels with you until it doesn't work.'

"They didn't get off the curbing. I went by'em. I ended up with three or four Chiefs

with blue tanks, "B" motors that Crocker sold. And we'd all go by—pop the pipes at'em, button it (shut off the ignition) and load'em, and let go and bang'em, and nobody got off the curbing—*nobody*. I mean, they thought I was insane, which I *was*. You know, I mean they're dealing with an insane character, 'cause they're *tough*, brother. These guys were everything from second story men on down. One of 'em was indited for murder, and everything else—High Warden.

"But we had fun.... I—Crocker—sold quite a few sports motorcycles. Until that time almost everything was commercial—vans and stuff. And then I was offered a job to take this bankrupt Indian agency over in Indianapolis, and went up there. I had the fun of outselling John Morgan by registration figures in Marion county, and Harley took his agency away from him 'cause Indian dealers *didn't* outsell Harley dealers. They're a sales-oriented outfit. Indian was engineering—spent their money changing the bike and Harley would wait three or four years and copy it. In my opinion, all Harley would change was the headlight and muffler each year, or toolbox, and (then) they had a new model. It was the same old road oiler they had before. All the oil went in the primary side and went out the back. I wouldn't ride behind a Harley 'cause I'd get oil splattered."

**Chief, 1924**
Indian favored the Scout with most of their advertising effort, feeling the small twin was better at recruiting people into motorcycling. However, from its inception as a 60.88ci, 998cc version, the Chief rivaled the Scout in sales.

When an alternative 73.6ci, 1206cc Big Chief was offered in 1923, the Big Chief assumed sales leadership. This mid-1924 example shows the new midseason pull-action front fork that replaced the earlier push-action fork. *Hill/Bentley*

*Previous pages*
**Indian show display, 1924**
The 1924 models on display early in the sales season. In midseason, both the Scout and Chief got new front forks. On the table was a scale model of the Indian factory. *Bob Finn*

**Standard, 1924**
The Standard (formerly Powerplus) models were last offered in the 1924 season. *Hill/Bentley*

**Gene Walker and four-valve single, 1924**
In an effort to reduce accidents, all 1924 national championship racing was done with 30.50ci, 500cc motors. Factory rider Gene Walker responded to this rule change by campaigning a four-valve single dating back to the Oscar Hedstrom days, but with an updated frame tailored to dirt-track requirements. Walker was the standout racer in short events, where all-out racing skill wasn't diluted by team strategy and the threat of breakdowns. Despite the move to smaller racing motors, flat-track racing remained deadly in an era when helmets and medical support were primitive. Walker was killed while practicing for a 1924 race. A winner of nineteen national titles during his six-year career, his loss was keenly felt. *Maldwyn Jones collection*

**Orie Steele and Scout, circa 1924**
One of Indian's rising competition stars was Orie Steele, who became the preeminent hillclimber during the late 1920s. Here, early in his career, he's surrounded by some of the trophies won with his Scout hillclimber. *EMAP archives*

**Prince, 1925**
For 1925, Indian again championed the causes of economy and learning ease, by offering the 21.35ci, 350cc side-valve Prince single. However, the wedge-shape tank, similar to those on English lightweights, proved unpopular. Clutch action was by a left-hand lever, which must have caused some problems with the left-hand throttle.

**Indian dealership, 1925**
A typical smalltown Indian dealership.
*Hill/Bentley*

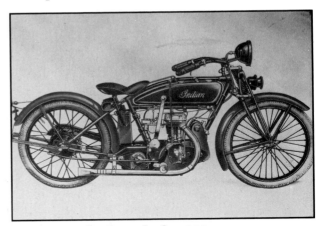

**Prince gets the Scout look, 1926**
On the Prince, the unsightly wedge-shape tank was dropped in 1926, in favor of the Scout look. *Bob Finn*

*Right*
**Scout, 1925**
With toe to the ground, advertising department staffer Ralph Houseman was captured by the advertising department camera. The 1925 Scout and Prince introduced removable cylinder heads to the Indian line. *Bob Finn*

**Paul Anderson and new eight-valve twin, 1925**
At Arpajon, France, in 1925, Paul Anderson rode a new eight-valve twin to a claimed speed of more than 159mph! After running about 112mph in the opposite direction (heck of a head wind!), his claimed record was more than 135mph, a speed unsurpassed as a world record until 1930. However, questions about the timing device prevented official recognition of the Anderson runs. *EMAP archives*

**Paul Anderson and new eight-valve twin, 1925**
Anderson also made some sidecar runs. This view clearly shows this is a new eight-valve instead of the old Hedstrom eight-valve. *EMAP archives*

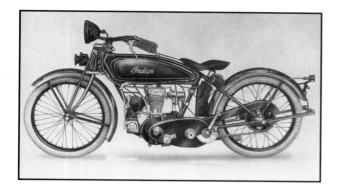

**Prince, 1926**
Detail changes on the 1926 Prince included a new chainguard that wrapped around the rear sprocket. *Bob Finn*

*Below*

**Prince, 1926**
Indian pitched the Prince as a practical transportation alternative to the automobile. This publicity photo suggests the Prince could go deep into the woods to find your favorite hunting area. The man with the gun is Carl White, road tester and service man. *Bob Finn*

**Prince overhead-valve, 1926**
An overhead-valve Prince was
offered in 1926. During the 1926
season, all Indians were first
available with unpainted
crankcases, as in this example.
*Hill/Bentley*

**Prince overhead-valve, 1926**
Another look at the overhead-valve Prince.
*Hill/Bentley*

# Color Gallery

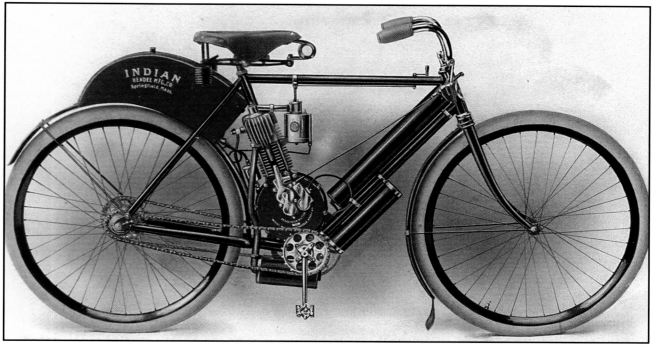

**Diamond-frame single, 1904**
Right-hand twist-grip ignition control was introduced in 1904. Speed control was by the ignition lever, and the left-hand throttle was infrequently used, such as when approaching a hill. Claimed output was 1.75hp, enough to propel the 98lb machine to more than 30mph. Mandatory dry-cell battery ignition was good for 800 to 2,500 miles, and the battery was described as "the best brains can produce." *Hill/Bentley*

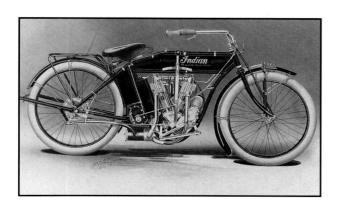

**TT twin, 1912**
Capitalizing on its 1911 Isle of Man TT victory, Indian offered for 1912 a pair of TT models. This was the 60.92ci, 998cc TT twin with two-speed transmission. The new right-side clutch lever location simplified coordination with the left-hand throttle. Dual rear brakes were fitted to the TT models. *Hill/Bentley*

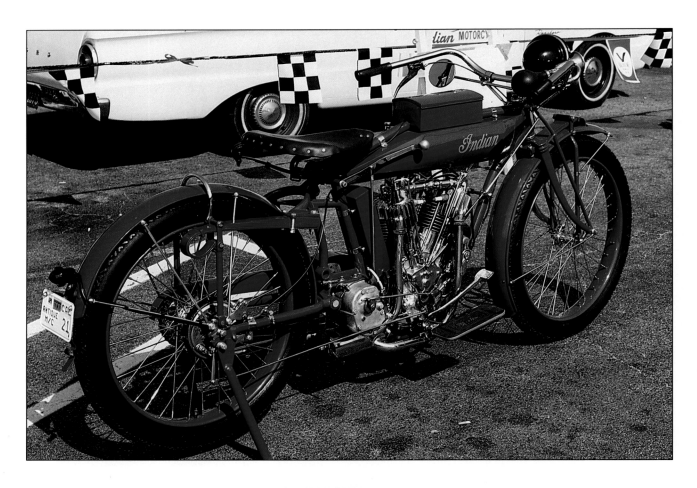

**F-head twin, 1915**
A 1915 F-head twin. Restoration by Dewey Bonkrud.

**F-head twin motor, 1915**
The 1915 motor produced a claimed 10hp. These machines could be cruised above 50mph, though most roads weren't safe enough for long stretches at such fast speeds. *Bonkrud*

**F-head twin motor, 1915**
By 1915, sporty big twins were the main emphasis on showroom floors because low-cost Ford cars were rapidly displacing motorcycles as mere transportation devices. *Bonkrud*

**Dewey Bonkrud and F-head twin, 1915**
This photo of the late Dewey Bonkrud also represents the antique motorcycle shows conducted on California mall parking lots for a number of years. Note the tall-in-the-saddle riding position of the early Indians.

**Indian tank logo, circa 1915**
For a brief period, Indian operated a factory in Toronto, Canada, as attested by the tank of this unrestored twin. This was a true factory, not just an assembly site.

*Below*
**Small-base eight-valve twin, circa 1916**
Left side of a small-base eight-valve. Restoration by Stephen Wright.

**Small-base eight-valve twin, circa 1916**
One of the fabulous small-base eight-valve racers that dominated United States motordromes. Restoration by Stephen Wright. *Sam Hotton*

**Four-valve single, circa 1916**
For local-interest racing on half-mile tracks, the Indian mainstays for several years were four-valve singles. Each was essentially half of an eight-valve twin. This unrestored example, owned by the late Russ Harmon, looks more like the racers did in their day because of the considerable oil loss through slits cut in the cylinders. These were called "ported" engines.

**Daytona frame twin, 1920**
The Daytona frame was introduced by Indian about 1920. The main difference from the Marion frame was a pronounced curvature of the tube under the seat. Restoration by Stephen Wright. *Sam Hotton*

**Powerplus, 1920**

Detail changes on the 1920 Powerplus included new handlebars, screw-down fork lubricators, new headlight, larger inlet and exhaust valves, larger exhaust ports, and new Splitdorf Aero magneto. Said the 1920 catalog: "To improve the rugged Powerplus would seem superfluous to its army of satisfied riders, but in view of the constant advances in metallurgy, engineering, and manufacturing, Indian is unwilling to withhold from it patrons the benefits of such progress. The results of intensive experience in meeting United States and Allied Government demands in the World War are manifested as new and outstanding features in the improved Powerplus...." *Hill/Bentley*

# *Indian Chief*

### PRICE $435

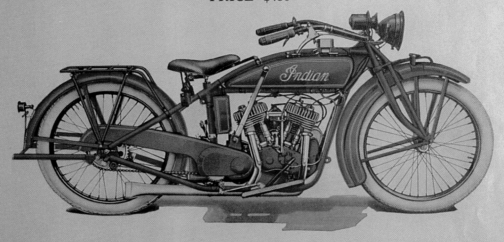

WHILE the INDIAN CHIEF was designed primarily to meet the requirements of sidecar service, nevertheless, as a solo mount where the qualities of power, speed and stamina are required, the INDIAN CHIEF has already been highly praised for the ease with which it is handled.

Besides embodying the highly desirable features of the SCOUT in increased proportions, the INDIAN CHIEF incorporates several notable refinements. The cylinders of its Powerplus Motor have been provided with additional cooling flanges. The mud-guards are the new INDIAN Crowned type. The generator is driven by a spur gear, enclosed with the timing gear train, and is compactly housed at the forward end of the crankcase. A battery of increased capacity is provided, most conveniently located. The saddle is mounted on the new INDIAN spring seat-post. A new type Splitdorf Magneto embodying several decided advantages is standard equipment.

BATTERY CASE

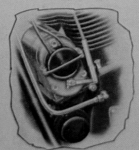

MAGNETO AND GENERATOR

**120mph plus, 1928**
In 1928, Indian campaigned the 45 overhead on the boards. On the Rockingham, New Hampshire, one-mile boardtrack these machines consistently hit peak speeds of 120-122mph. *Chuck Vernon*

*Left*
**Overhead-valve 45ci racer, 1926**
The Chuck Vernon 45ci, 750cc (nominal) racer outfitted for road racing. Twenty-six of the 45ci overhead-valve racers were built in 1926. Most were used for hillclimbing. *Chuck Vernon*

*Far left*
**Chief ad, 1922**
The new 61ci (nominal), 1000cc, Chief was the headline act of the 1922 season. *Dick and Rita Sanchez collection*

**Ace, 1927**
For most of the first three decades of American motorcycle sport, one or more motorcycle magazines were published either weekly or biweekly. This issue highlights the new Indian Ace. *George and Milli Yarocki*

**101 Scout, 1929**
The Model 101 Scout was
introduced in mid-1928 as a
1929 model, according to the
parts books. This is a mid- to
late-1929 model. Restoration by
Gene Grimes.

**101 Scout, 1929**
You can bet on this: 101 Scout
motors rarely looked this good
in their day—they were usually
covered with oil mist and road
dust. Restoration by Gene
Grimes.

**101 Scout, 1929**
Left side of the Model 101 Scout motor. Restoration by Gene Grimes.

**Max Bubeck and Four, 1930**
Max Bubeck proudly shows off his 1930 Four, since sold. In the late 1980s, Bubeck put more than 30,000 trouble-free miles on this machine at 60–70mph cruising speeds, thanks to an oil cooler, filter, and crankshaft drilled with extra oil passages. Restoration by Max Bubeck.

**Four, 1930**
Closeup of the Bubeck 1930
Four. Restoration by Max
Bubeck.

*Below*
**Four, 1936**
Among Indian's bigger mistakes,
one would have to list the 1936
and 1937 "upside-down" Fours,
so named because the valve
configuration was reversed.

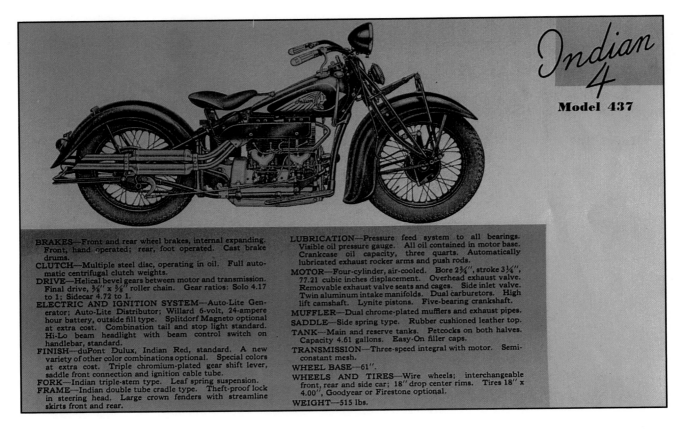

*Indian 4*

**Model 437**

BRAKES—Front and rear wheel brakes, internal expanding. Front, hand operated; rear, foot operated. Cast brake drums.

CLUTCH—Multiple steel disc, operating in oil. Full automatic centrifugal clutch weights.

DRIVE—Helical bevel gears between motor and transmission. Final drive, ⅜" x ⅝" roller chain. Gear ratios: Solo 4.17 to 1; Sidecar 4.72 to 1.

ELECTRIC AND IGNITION SYSTEM—Auto-Lite Generator; Auto-Lite Distributor; Willard 6-volt, 24-ampere hour battery, outside fill type. Splitdorf Magneto optional at extra cost. Combination tail and stop light standard. Hi-Lo beam headlight with beam control switch on handlebar, standard.

FINISH—duPont Dulux, Indian Red, standard. A new variety of other color combinations optional. Special colors at extra cost. Triple chromium-plated gear shift lever, saddle front connection and ignition cable tube.

FORK—Indian triple-stem type. Leaf spring suspension.

FRAME—Indian double tube cradle type. Theft-proof lock in steering head. Large crown fenders with streamline skirts front and rear.

LUBRICATION—Pressure feed system to all bearings. Visible oil pressure gauge. All oil contained in motor base. Crankcase oil capacity, three quarts. Automatically lubricated exhaust rocker arms and push rods.

MOTOR—Four-cylinder, air-cooled. Bore 2¾", stroke 3¼", 77.21 cubic inches displacement. Overhead exhaust valve. Removable exhaust valve seats and cages. Side inlet valve. Twin aluminum intake manifolds. Dual carburetors. High lift camshaft. Lynite pistons. Five-bearing crankshaft.

MUFFLER—Dual chrome-plated mufflers and exhaust pipes.

SADDLE—Side spring type. Rubber cushioned leather top.

TANK—Main and reserve tanks. Petcocks on both halves. Capacity 4.61 gallons. Easy-On filler caps.

TRANSMISSION—Three-speed integral with motor. Semi-constant mesh.

WHEEL BASE—61".

WHEELS AND TIRES—Wire wheels; interchangeable front, rear and side car; 18" drop center rims. Tires 18" x 4.00", Goodyear or Firestone optional.

WEIGHT—515 lbs.

**Four, 1937**

A 1937 twin-carburetor "upside-down" Four model. The overhead exhaust valves and side inlet valves produced more power, and heat dissipation was better because of the large cylinder head area in close proximity to the exhaust ports. But the appearance—ugh! *From the H. J. Norman collection, copy photo by Bill Ellington*

**Harold Mathewson, 1991**
At a banquet honoring his induction into the Indian Motocycle Hall of Fame, former hillclimbing star Harold

Mathewson sits astride his factory-produced circa 1936 hillclimber built around a Sport Scout motor. *Ella Hatfield*

**Chief, 1937**
This 1937 Chief shows the new forward gearshift location. This machine has been updated for practicality and does not feature the original "T" oil lines that were prone to leak. The machine's owner and restorer are unknown by the author.

**Four, 1938**
Restoration expert Elmer Lower shows off his 1938 Four. Restoration by Elmer Lower.

**Four, 1938**
The Elmer Lower Four.

**Four, 1938**
Closeup of the Lower 1938
Four. The new 1938 motor
featured cylinders cast in pairs
and totally enclosed valve gear.

**Prince prototype, 1926**
This experimental overhead-cam Prince was road tested during 1926. *Bob Finn*

**Prince prototype, 1926**
The overhead-cam Prince probably was inspired by the success of the English overhead-cam Velocette, which made its debut as a 1925 model. *Emmett Moore collection*

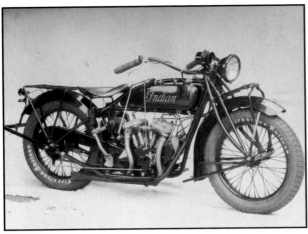

**Scout, 1926**
Detail changes on the 1926 Scouts included a new method of mounting the exhaust pipes. This example has the traditional painted crankcases, primary drive cover, and transmission, but dealers and riders could specify these parts unpainted. *Bob Finn*

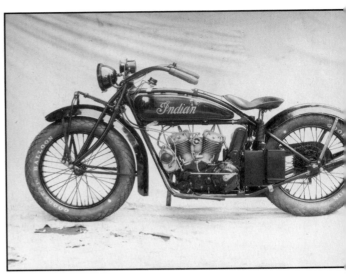

**Scout, 1926**
Large so-called balloon tires became optional on Scouts during mid-1925. *Finn*

**The Armstrongs, circa 1926**
These ice frolickers are members of one of Indian's "royal" families. In the sidecar is Erle "Red" Armstrong, later known as "Pop." On the motorcycle is his son Bob. *Maldwyn Jones*

**Chief with sidecar, 1926**
As ever, the sidecar suitability of the Chief was stressed. New features included new handlebars, a new rear brake, and more tilt to the footboards. *Bob Finn*

**Indian show display, 1926**
Scene from the January 1926 New York City motorcycle show. A white overhead-valve Prince Sport was in the foreground as a raffle prize. *Bob Finn*

**Living it up, circa 1926**
A summer day and a new Prince. What more could a young man want? Well, OK, a girl maybe. *Hill/Bentley*

**Johnny Seymour and four-valve
single, circa 1926**
Rider Johnny Seymour on a four-valve 30.50ci,
500cc single. On this machine, or one like it,
Seymour set an American record of 115mph at
Daytona in early 1926. *Maldwyn Jones collection*

**M. L. "Curly" Fredericks and
"Altoona" twin, 1928**
Although this photo was taken in 1928, both the
rider and motorcycle made greater history at this
same track in 1926. M. L. "Curly" Fredericks is
shown on the motorcycle—or one just like it—
with which he rode the all-time fastest board-
track lap, 120.3mph at the Rockingham 1-mile
track in Salem, New Hampshire. The motor is a
60.88ci, 998cc Chief derivative, and features twin
Zenith carburetors. Indian called these Altoona
motors, in honor of some racing success on the
Altoona, Pennsylvania, board track. *Maldwyn
Jones collection*

**Sprouts Elder and four-valve
single, circa 1926**
The Johnny Seymour-style
four-valve 30.50ci, 500cc racers
were used throughout the
1920s. The rider is Sprouts
Elder, who later gained
international fame as the
father of speedway racing.
"Speedway" is used here in
the modern sense of flat
tracking on cinders. *Emmett
Moore collection*

**Forty-Five overhead-valve twin, 1926**
Concurrent with side-valve racing development, Indian followed the more conventional formula of increasing power output by putting all valves upstairs. In 1926, twenty-six 45ci, 750cc overhead-valve twins were built to compete in the newly established 45ci class. A 45ci class was made obligatory by the Excelsior-Henderson company's sales success with its recently launched Super-X 45ci road model. Restoration by Chuck Vernon.

**Forty-Five overhead-valve twin, 1926**
Another view of the 45ci overhead-valve hillclimber. Restoration by Chuck Vernon.

**Customized Prince, 1927**
Even little machines were customized in the 1920s. This is a 1926 model 21.35ci, 350cc overhead-valve Prince, updated with a 1927 belt-driven generator. Both low and high bars were popular on customs, but shortened fenders were almost always selected by customizers. *Ed Kretz*

**Ace four, 1927**
Indian bought out the Ace company just in time for the January-February 1927 motorcycle show in New York City's Madison Square Garden. The Ace was the brainchild of William Henderson, who had earlier produced the Henderson marque. Bill Henderson always favored overhead inlet and side exhaust valves. He probably became disenchanted with the Henderson motorcycle situation after the American Excelsior firm (no connection with the British Excelsior) bought him out and put all the Henderson's valves on the side. *Hill/Bentley*

**Indian show display, 1927**
Sharing the spotlight with the Ace was a new 45ci, 750cc Scout dubbed the Police Special. In those days, police motorcycles were built like racing machines, with looser clearances that provided extra speed at the expense of added mechanical noise. The new "Forty-Five" (they were never called "Four-Fives" back then) was promoted as a fast, yet agile machine—and they were. *Hill/Bentley*

**Scout Police Special, 1927**
The new 45ci, 750cc twin was termed the Police Special in advertisements, but the tank legend read "Scout 45." *Hill/Bentley*

**Indian Service School, 1927**
A typical Service School class.
The arrow and label "me"
points out Fred Marsh. The man
standing has his left hand on
instructor Erle "Red" Armstrong.
The first factory Service School
opened in 1923. *Fred Marsh*

**Roots of the street cruiser genre, 1927**
The roots of today's ideas about how a street
cruiser should look. Before hillclimbing became
popular, most stripped-down customs were given
the low look like the Prince custom job shown
earlier. Hillclimbers were the beginning of the
new "in" look. *Hill/Bentley*

**Ace four and customized Powerplus, 1927**
San Francisco Indian dealers. The year was probably 1927 because of the new Ace—not an "Indian Ace," which came out in 1928. The Powerplus custom shows the newly popular styling inspired by hillclimbers. *Hill/Bentley*

**Road riding, 1927**
Oddly, you could buy Mobil Oil at this Texaco station. The cart with three pumps is for kerosene (paraffin in British usage). This photo was included in the 1928 Indian sales catalog. Driver of the sidecar outfit is Norm Turner, factory salesman and district manager in the Ohio area. *Hill/Bentley*

**Chief, circa 1928**
A circa 1928 Chief and sidecar
provided an ideal patrol unit in
this mountainous terrain. *Finn*

**Chief, 1928**
At the time of the restoration of this Chief, larger
tires weren't available for restoration projects.
Because the Chief was emphasized as a sidecar
machine, the left-side kickstarter was standard
from 1922 through 1931. Restoration by Ernie
Skelton. *George Hays*

**Styles of racers, circa 1928**
Second from the right in this lineup of Indian racers is Fred Marsh. Class A factory-supported racing permitted extensive modifications and any kind of fuel. The racing machine on the left has a frame from the eight-valve era, while the other motorcycles are Prince derivatives. *Fred Marsh*

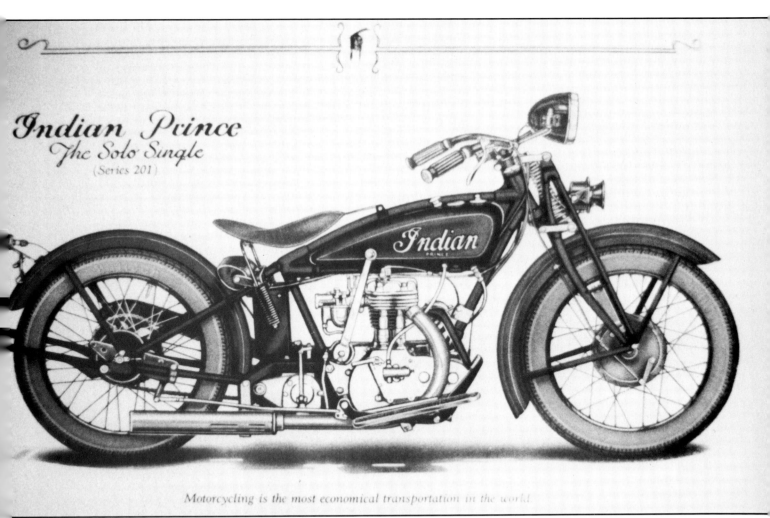

*Indian Prince*
*The Solo Single*
(Series 201)

*Indian*
PRINCE

*Motorcycling is the most economical transportation in the world.*

**Prince, 1928**
The Prince got a shapelier tank and new muffler in 1928. This was the last year of the little single. *George and Milli Yarocki*

**Jim Davis and "Altoona" twin, 1928**
At the Rockingham board track in Salem, New Hampshire, Jim Davis joined Curly Fredericks in racing an Altoona twin. *Maldwyn Jones collection*

**Indian show display, 1928**
A display of 1928 models in Belgium. In the left foreground is an advertisement for the spectacularly unsuccessful Indian shock absorber, which the factory tried to sell as an automobile accessory. In the left background, a four-valve racer is displayed, while in the right foreground a Scout 45 poster is prominent. The two pseudo Indian men don't look happy with their roles! *Hill/Bentley*

**101 Scout, 1928**
Introduced in the spring of 1928, the Model 101 Scouts were about 3in longer and 1in lower at the saddle. As the original Indian caption read, "At left is right quartering view of the New Scout depicting 'Bullet Type' head lamp, front brake and control and new generator location; center, showing comfortable riding position as seen from ahead; right, left quartering view indicating horn and general sturdy construction. Big balloon tires on all the Series." The man in the middle is advertising department staffer Ralph Houseman. *George and Milli Yarocki*

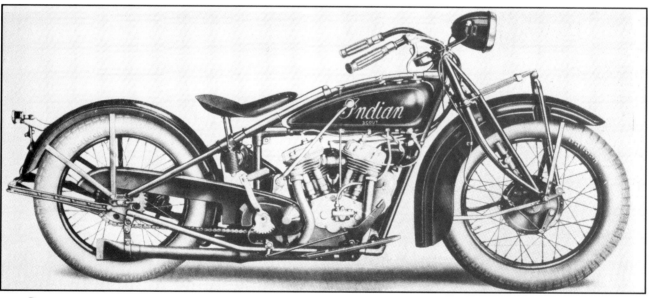

**101 Scout, 1928**
As the original Indian caption read, "The right hand view of Series 101 Scout shows speedy lines, new 'Bullet Type' headlight and grip-lever for front brake and brake itself. Generator is seen behind seat mast." *George and Milli Yarocki*

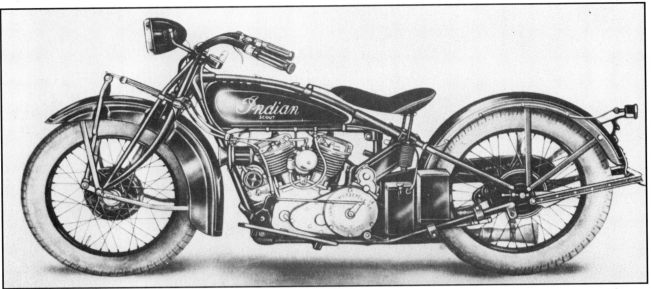

**101 Scout, 1928**
As the original Indian caption read, "Showing the fine rakish lines of the New Scout as seen from the left. This shows to advantage the balloon tires, new location of battery box and generator drive and sturdy brace at crown for mudguard." *George and Milli Yarocki*

**101 Scout, 1928**
Closeup of a Scout motor shows the larger cases that provided a through-bolt motor-mounting system that replaced the front motor plates beginning with the 1927 45 ci Police Specials. The artist's retouching on the motor mount area is slightly off. *Finn*

**101 Scout, 1929**
Indian advertising continually worked over the
Native American theme. Here, the chief was
perhaps conveying the message that the 101 has
a 57 1/8in wheelbase compared to the earlier
Scouts at 54in. The unusual carburetor is a
Tillotson. *Hill/Bentley*

**"Chout" custom, circa 1929**
The new 101 frame inspired a number of Indian
sport riders to shoehorn in a Chief engine, thus
producing a Chout, hybrid of a Chief and Scout.
Though shown here to represent the genesis of
the Chout idea, several years passed before old
101 Scouts were cheap and plentiful enough to
see Chouts become popular. *Hill/Bentley*

**101 Scout racer, circa 1930**
101 Scouts were almost immediately pressed into service for amateur racing. The rider is Harrison Reno. *Hill/Bentley*

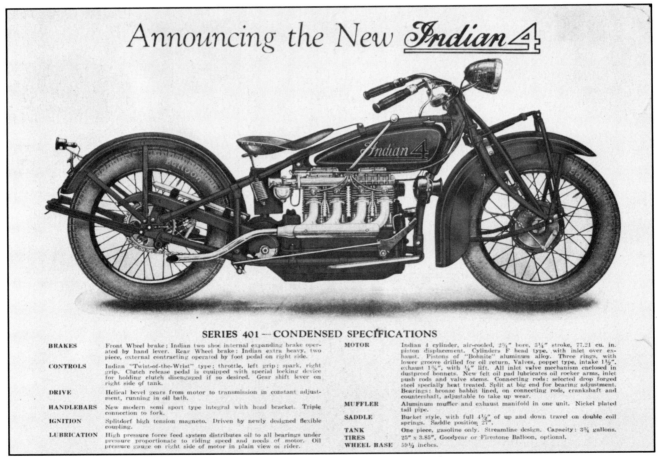

## Announcing the New *Indian 4*

### SERIES 401 — CONDENSED SPECIFICATIONS

| | |
|---|---|
| **BRAKES** | Front Wheel brake; Indian two shoe internal expanding brake operated by hand lever. Rear Wheel brake; Indian extra heavy, two piece, external contracting operated by foot pedal on right side. |
| **CONTROLS** | Indian "Twist-of-the-Wrist" type; throttle, left grip; spark, right grip. Clutch release pedal is equipped with special locking device for holding clutch disengaged if so desired. Gear shift lever on right side of tank. |
| **DRIVE** | Helical bevel gears from motor to transmission in constant adjustment, running in oil bath. |
| **HANDLEBARS** | New modern semi sport type integral with head bracket. Triple connection to fork. |
| **IGNITION** | Splitdorf high tension magneto. Driven by newly designed flexible coupling. |
| **LUBRICATION** | High pressure force feed system distributes oil to all bearings under pressure proportionate to riding speed and needs of motor. Oil pressure gauge on right side of motor in plain view of rider. |

| | |
|---|---|
| **MOTOR** | Indian 4 cylinder, air-cooled, 2⅝" bore, 2¼" stroke, 77.21 cu. in. piston displacement. Cylinders F head type, with inlet over exhaust. Pistons of "Bohnite" aluminum alloy. Three rings, with lower groove drilled for oil return. Valves, poppet type, intake 1½", exhaust 1⅜", with ¼" lift. All inlet valve mechanism enclosed in dustproof bonnets. New felt oil pad lubricates oil rocker arms, inlet push rods and valve stems. Connecting rods; selected drop forged steel specially heat treated. Split at big end for bearing adjustment. Bearings; bronze babbit lined, on connecting rods, crankshaft and countershaft, adjustable to take up wear. |
| **MUFFLER** | Aluminum muffler and exhaust manifold in one unit. Nickel plated tail pipe. |
| **SADDLE** | Bucket style, with full 4½" of up and down travel on double coil springs. Saddle position 27". |
| **TANK** | One piece, gasoline only. Streamline design. Capacity: 3¾ gallons. |
| **TIRES** | 25" x 3.85", Goodyear or Firestone Balloon, optional. |
| **WHEEL BASE** | 59½ inches. |

**Four, Model 401, 1929**
Announced in August 1928, the new Model 401 combined the Ace engine with a front fork and frame that mimicked the popular 101 Scout frame. Model 101 frame tubes were not used, however, as larger-diameter tubing was in order. The 101 tank tooling was used to produce the Model 401 tank. *George and Milli Yarocki*

**Fred Marsh and Prince, circa 1929**
Fred Marsh of Hartford, Connecticut, aboard a Prince derivative flat tracker. This motorcycle was raced for several more years as part of the Marsh stable. Indian staffer Matt Keevers used it in 1936 night speedway races. By 1992, Marsh was the oldest former Indian dealer, and in fact, still was running a motorcycle shop. *Fred Marsh*

**Four, Model 401, 1929**
Unlike the 1932 and later Indian Fours, the Fours of late 1928 through 1931 were compact. In fact, these Fours and the 101 Scouts had the same wheelbase. The rider was Hap Alzina, a distributor who kept West Coast Indian sales above the national average. The Ace-style single front downtube was retained. *Hill/Bentley*

## Non-motorcycle Products Fail
### *Over One Million Dollars Lost*

"During 1928 and 1929 the company engaged itself in the manufacture and distribution of lines not directly related to its principal products. These so-called unrelated lines included outboard motors, shock-absorbers, electric refrigerators, ventilators and automobiles, and the engaging in the manufacture and sale of these lines resulted in a decrease in the working capital position of the company of approximately $1,250,000. In the closing months of 1929 the production of unrelated lines was discontinued.... "

*Retrospective, From A Report Presented In April 1941*

**Indian show display, 1929**
This display of 1929 models included a 101 Scout with two-color tank. On the back wall, a poster brags about Johnny Seymour's 1926 records at Daytona Beach. *Hill/Bentley*

**Four, 1929**
Late 1929 Fours got a new double front downtube frame, as shown on this 1930 Four, which reduced vibration. The less attractive left side of Fours was generally not shown in sales literature. *Max Bubeck*

*Below*
**Bob Armstrong, 1929**
Bob Armstrong, son of Erle, tries unsuccessfully to put on a happy face after sharing around-the-clock driving from the Midwest to Massachusetts. Using this 80ci, 1300cc machine, young Armstrong was the top amateur hillclimber of 1929. *Emmett Moore collection*

*Chapter 5*

# 1930–1939

## *Du Pont to the Rescue*

In the spring of 1930, E. Paul du Pont, one of *the* du Ponts of Delaware, sold the controlling interest in the Du Pont automobile company to Indian and also bought a large block of Indian stock. Although Indian was financially weak, the company had considerable excess factory capaci-

**Chief, 1930**
Cast-aluminum tanks were featured on the 1930 Chiefs, but not on the Scouts and Fours; however, they proved either unsatisfactory or too costly. The remaining stocks of cast tanks were used up on the first few 1931 model Chiefs, and built-up tanks were fitted thereafter. Restoration by Gene Grimes.

ty, a strong dealer network, and had enjoyed recent steady sales growth. E. Paul du Pont quickly concluded that some Indian directors had been passing company money around under the table, the payments being thinly disguised as consulting fees. Armed with legal counsel, he forced management to open the financial records for his review. He learned that the company had been slow paying its debts and that many of Indian's suppliers would sell to Indian on a cash basis only. Du Pont pressed his attack and was able to buy out the previous management team at a low price as the management feared legal prosecution if du Pont didn't get his way.

To run the Indian company's day-to-day affairs, du Pont brought in Loring F. "Joe" Hosley, former production manager at Du Pont Motors, builders of the Du Pont automobile. Production methods were changed to reduce the dependence on a large materials inventory. Overhead and operating expenses were substantially reduced.

Du Pont took an active interest in the company's engineering problems. He kept a stable of Indian models at his estate and provided written reports on deficiencies. He even studied engineering drawings and made suggestions.

Despite improvements in management and motorcycle design, by 1933 the company was down to operating at only 5 percent of plant capacity. At one point, there wasn't sufficient money to meet the payroll, so a hurry-up loan was obtained from a local bank. A series of paycuts and layoffs ensured that there would be enough money to pay those employees still onboard. Du Pont considered filing for bankruptcy, then dropped the idea in favor of financial reorganization.

One of the casualties of the money crisis was the 101 Scout, so beloved of dealers and the most knowledgeable riders. When the decision was made to trim the 1932 model line to save money, the 101 Scout was eliminated. Although popular, the Scout was about as expensive to manufacture as the Chief, so the Scout probably couldn't command a sufficiently high sales price to cover its own costs.

Engineering and styling progress continued despite financial difficulties. In 1933, dry-sump (recirculating) lubrication replaced the traditional total-loss setup; Harley-Davidson didn't go completely over to dry-sump lubrication until four years later.

Du Pont's family connections enabled Indian to buy paint cheaply, which resulted in an explosion of color options. The "color war" with Harley-Davidson reached its zenith in 1934, when Indian listed twenty-four standard one- and two-color options, plus the extra-cost option of *any* nonlisted colors available in Du Pont paints.

In 1934, the new Sport Scout had the look of a sleek racer. It was based on the 45ci engine with a keystone frame and new flowing fenders. In 1935, the Chief and Four got streamlined fenders, and the Chief and Sport Scout were offered with optional four-speed transmissions. Feature by feature, the 1935 Indian lineup had it all over the Harley-Davidson lineup.

However, two bad product decisions were made in the 1930s, both involving the Four. The first of these mistakes was the 1936 "upside-down" Four, an ugly duckling and sales disaster that lingered one more year with minor improvements. With the worst sort of timing for Indian, in 1936 Harley-Davidson launched its 61ci overhead-valve twin, which became a sales leader and long-run hit. Indian's second mistake of this era was the 1938 Four, not so much because it needed a little more engineering to match its classic beauty, but because the development time and money would have paid off better in designing an overhead-valve big twin—which the bulk of American riders preferred.

Still, Indian's racing fortunes had revived with the new Class C (stock). From 1934 through 1938, Indian won most of the prestigious races such as the Daytona 200, the Laconia 100, the Langhorne 100, and the Springfield (Illinois) 25.

What of the all-important bottom line? Small profits from 1936 through 1939 weren't enough to offset huge losses earlier. From 1931 (1930 records are unavailable) through 1939, Indian lost a cumulative $1.4 million. Still, the du Pont-Hosley team had saved Indian.

*The author is indebted to the Research Center, Henry Ford Museum & Greenfield Village, for the use of the E. Paul du Pont Papers. All du Pont correspondence in this book is cited to "E. Paul du Pont Papers, Research Center, Henry Ford Museum & Greenfield Village."*

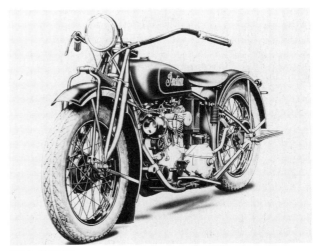

**Chief 1930**
The Klaxon horns were last used on 1930 models. *Hill/Bentley*

# Du Pont Takes Over

When E. Paul du Pont bought a substantial amount of Indian stock in April 1930, production rates had climbed rapidly, from 285 in December 1929 to 1,451 in March 1930. Police sales had improved markedly over the period.

But du Pont soon learned that the Indian Motocycle Company was several months behind in its credit payments and that many suppliers were dealing with Indian on a strictly cash basis. Considerable money had been lost in diversification efforts such as an automobile shock absorber, an automobile ventilator, and outboard motors. A series of deals suggested that the management was primarily interested in pumping up the value of their stock holdings by optimistic and misleading press releases, in order to bail out at the right time and leave others holding the bag.

It also appeared that company funds were being distributed under the table among certain board members. Stock records indicated that a block of stock valued at $106,000 had been issued—for cash, in du Pont's opinion—but the money was not to be found.

Du Pont was able to buy cheaply the additional shares needed to take control, by implying criminal action might be taken against the existing board if they did not exit Indian on his terms. Thus, du Pont insured himself against any legal action that might be forthcoming as a result of the previous administration.

INDIAN NEWS..MARCH, 1931

NOTE: The ancient motocycle, part of which is shown in the picture at left, is a 1902 INDIAN which now rests in the Smithsonian Institute at Washington

Loring F. Hosley
Vice-President and General Manager

E. Paul duPont
President

James A. Wright
Director of Sales and Advertising

Frederick W. Fisher
Factory Superintendent

Thomas M. Darrah
Secretary and Treasurer

Charles B. Franklin
Chief Engineer

INDIAN EXECUTIVES OF TODAY

GREAT men conceive ideas—spend years shaping them into successful industries—then pass the torch to other hands.

So it has been at Indian. The men who helped to found the Indian so many years ago have retired, and their tasks have been taken over by some of the men shown on this page.

These men—and every other man in the Indian Organization —even to the faraway corners of the globe—appreciate the mighty work done by the pioneers of earlier days. They have a keen realization of the responsibility which lies with every man at an Indian post today, and they are determined that as the years roll by—more Indians and finer Indians shall go forth from the Wigwam.

Theirs is the task of carrying on the great work begun by the founder of Indian—Thirty

# E. Paul du Pont Letters

As a financier with interests beyond the Indian Motocycle Company, E. Paul du Pont had no intention of taking over the direct management of Indian affairs. For this purpose he transferred from Du Pont Motors Company to Indian Mr. Loring F. "Joe" Hosley, who had been general manager of Du Pont Motors. But du Pont was indeed interested in motorcycles, having built one himself as a young man, and he was interested in engineering. For these reasons, as well as keeping abreast of the company's business progress, du Pont initiated a series of detailed monthly letters to Hosley. Some of these letters to Hosley, Hosley's letters to du Pont and other du Pont correspondence, will be presented.

**Harold Mathewson and Scout, circa 1930**
Rough and tumble hillclimbing was the rage
in the 1930s. Hillclimbing may have benefited
from the fact that AMA racing was limited to
relatively unpopular 21.35ci, 350cc and 30.50ci,
500cc single-cylinder Indians and Harley-
Davidsons, while the climbs continued to
showcase Americans' favorite type, the V-twin.
Manhandling this Scout was Harold Mathewson
of Fresno, California. *Harold Mathewson*

*Du Pont Letter to Hosley, August 21, 1930*

# Problems With The Chiefs

"I did not ask when I was there the last
time as to whether a project is on foot to go
right ahead and finish the new fly wheels
and aluminum pistons as last tried in the
Chief 74. I again urge that no time be lost,
and suggest that this machine be put on the
road and given a thorough test. Meanwhile,
finish all preliminaries necessary to getting
ready to supply this as soon as it is possible
to do it....

"We should also have fairly soon an
estimate of the cost of equipping the Chief
74 model with aluminum pistons and new
fly wheels, and scrapping all existing material and to include the rebuilding of assembled engines on the floor...."

# Du Pont Favors Harley 74 Over Chief

Comparing a 1930 Harley-Davidson 74 to a 1930 Indian Chief, du Pont wrote:

"1. On the general construction of the machine it appears that the Indian is much better, as having a double tube for the bottom of the frame with the running board attached to it, offers to my mind, a far stronger construction than the Harley scheme of attaching the running boards to the crank case.

"2. The vibration is very much less—so much less, in fact that the Harley is quite usable whereas the Indian Chief is not. To convince yourself of this, put the two machines side by side on a stand and start the motors. As they speed up, the Indian will be observed to vibrate so badly that it slides backward on the floor, and any attempt to hold it is painful to the hand; whereas the Harley stays more or less where it is placed at any engine speed.

"3. I notice that the gear ratio on the Harley is much lower than Indian, so much so that Harley is most unpleasant to ride at speeds under 40 or 50 miles an hour, and can hardly be run under 30.

"4. I believe the location of tool box and horn on the Harley-Davidson is better than on the Indian.

"5. The sitting position on the Harley is much more comfortable, but I observe no advantage in their spring seat post, nor could I observe any advantages in their riding qualities, and such Harley riders as there are around here are not particularly pleased with the riding qualities of the Harley.

"In general, I do not think our engineering is up to date in the matter of allowing our motors to churn up at maximum speed, and as high speed seems to be what is wanted, I think something might be done about this. On the other hand I discover that there are surprising numbers of accidents on motorcycles which are due to high speed, so it might be well to consider whether a much higher speed should be given or not. Our Wilmington dealer, Mr. VanSice, has fixed up a Scout machine to give high speed, and it is licking all the Harley-Davidson 74s in this vicinity."

**Herb Radmore and Four, 1930**
Chrome plating was first advertised in 1930 sales literature. Montreal dealer Herb Radmore lost little time in using the new technology to customize his Four. *Hill/Bentley*

**Four, 1931**
The last of the Fours with the between-the-rails tank was the 1931 model. The new internal-expanding rear brake was also used on other 1931 models. *Hill/Bentley*

*Du Pont Letter to H. Erickson of Minneapolis (stockholder), November 20, 1930*
## Chiefs, 4-Speed Transmission, Duco Finish, Dry Sump Oiling, Tanks

"...the new series of the Chief is only a step. We had on hand when I took charge of the Indian Company about three-fourths of a million dollars of inventory, a great part of which would have to be sacrificed if immediate changes were made. I considered it essentially necessary that the Chief should be made so that it would run without the terrible vibration that has existed in the older models, and am glad to report that this has been so well accomplished that every Chief sent out of the factory from now on will run with less vibration than the Scout, and I think better than any 74 twin on the market....

"Your remarks on the four speed transmission are also exceedingly interesting, and I wish to say that I will watch this very carefully. It is an improvement which could not be done immediately with the present inventory—probably not before next August at the best.

"As to the Duco finish, this has already been taken care of.

"Concerning the dry sump lubrication, we already have two machines on the road experimenting with this....

"...I am much interested in your stating that the tank on the Scout is the right thing, as our Sales Department reports that the two tanks concealing the frame in the Chief and the Harley-Davidson are the only thing, and that we must have this to be in the running. Personally, I don't like the idea, because the Scout type of tank is, from an engineering standpoint, far superior to the split tank and never gives trouble, whereas the split tank springs leaks.

"...You might be interested to know that I am an enthusiastic rider of the Scout and Chief and the 4, taking one one day and one the next instead of using our automobile every time that weather permits...."

# Dealer Complains About Chiefs

"...If there is any possible chance please give us a good 74 motor, and change the Chief to give it more speed, make the bottom of these motors so they will hold up. The crank pins, roller bearings, lower connecting rod bushings—it is fierce the way they go to pieces in no time.... I found with our Indians, motors get too hot and too much vibration; front and rear brakes, no good; forks, too rough riding.

"Mr. du Pont, I have been selling motorcycles for 19 years and I know what I am talking about; I sold the Harley-Davidson fourteen years in this territory, and I know what they are made of and how they stand up.... If the Indian factory made a good 74 motor I could put them in the City and also the County, but I can not put the Chiefs in; the County men rawhide their motors, and I know the Chiefs will not stand up; I would just lose my reputation if I sold them, so I don't on that account. The Four is mostly too high in price to sell to the City or County, although I have twelve Indian Fours on the St. Petersburg Police Department, but the officers there buy their own machines.

"Now what the Indian factory should do, is to make a 74 motor that will stand up, something to compete with the 74 Harley-Davidsons. I am fighting a battle here, and have got to have more weapons to fight with or give up, and I am one of the fellows that wants to die with his boots on.

"So please do all in your power to give us better production and especially on the Chief."

# Engineering, Sale of Half of Factory

"1. *General Engineering Program:*
I have asked Mr. Franklin to make up a complete list of every item which we have discussed in the Engineering Department and I will forward this to you as quickly as possible. I feel very sure that we must lay down a definite program at this time if we are to get things in tune.

"2. *Splitdorf Generator:*
I made the decision, today, not to go to the Aut Generator on the Chief but to continue the Splitdorf until the new model which will come out in August. If we do not do this it will mean, as you know, quite a scrappage on the present crankcases and also mean new pattern equipment at this time. This will no sooner get into effect than we will have to make another change for the dry sump in August....

"3. *Gasoline Tank....*

"4. *Sale of One-Half Present Factory:*
As I told you, we have rented a portion of the building the other side of the tracks to a carpet concern here, and we have already received our first month's rent, which will be $119 per month. This was rented thru a Mr. Clark, and last night he asked me if we would consider selling the portion of the plant which includes the offices back as far as the railroad track. This was an entirely new thought, but I know of no other thing that would make a greater saving for us. The prospective customer is the Tasty Yeast Company.... The sale of this portion of the plant would practically cut our fixed overhead, such as taxes, heat, maintenance, light, etc., about one-half. At any rate, this is food for thought and I will talk to you about it next time we meet.

**101 Scout, 1931**

The last 101 Scouts were the 1931 models, which featured a new headlight and mounting system, new muffler, and cadmium-plated spokes. A new oil pump varied output with throttle opening as well as engine speed. Still, riders were advised to use the hand pump for rough going. When the Model 101 was dropped from the 1932 lineup, many Indian dealers were upset because they regarded it as the best all-around model. However, the 101s didn't sell as well as the Chiefs. *Bob Finn*

---

*Du Pont Letter to Tony Motor Company, December 8, 1930*
# Du Pont Defends New Chiefs

"...As to the 74 motor, we have done all that can be done to the present motor without a complete redesigning, and believe that it is now a good machine. The vibration has been reduced to a point where it is better than the Scout, and some weak spots in the crankshaft have been eliminated which I believe was the cause of the bearings going to pieces.

"I am in hopes that you will find the new Chief o.k. I am not a fast rider myself, and do not abuse my machine, so am unable to say of my own knowledge against what rough usage they will stand up. Our testers at the factory report that they are now o.k. I have thrown all of the parts in the inventory which were faulty in the junk pile, and we are furnishing nothing but the new layout at present, which consists in better crank shaft and fly wheels, lighter pistons, different balance and greatly improved workmanship. I think if you will try one of the Chiefs that we are now producing you will be convinced, and I sincerely hope you will do so as I am anxious to hear reports from every one who is a judge of motorcycles as to whether what we have done is as good as I think it is."

**Scout overhead-valve, 1930–1933**
The Indian factory built a few overhead-valve Scout motors for 45ci, 750cc hillclimbing, and later, for 30.50ci, 500cc speedway racing, or short track as it was called in the United States. Later, the Al Crocker machine shop in Los Angeles built a similar motor for speedway racing. With Depression-era motorcycling a close-knit (OK, small) sport, a few special motors hung around for many years in the hands of a few top riders. Restoration by Chuck Vernon

*Du Pont Letter to Hosley, December 29, 1930*
# Traffic Car, Chief Shimmying, Allegheny Metal

"...I am very anxious to push the big traffic car, and would like to have a general arrangement tracing sent to me if this is possible.

"Please find out all you can and let me know about shimmying in motorcycles. This peculiar occurrence happened to our Chief. Paul was riding it on the Kennett Pike, travelling at a speed he estimates to have been 40 miles an hour. He took one hand off the handlebar to get a glove out of his pocket when it began to shimmy. The first two throws of the front wheel caused it to leap off the road fairly high into the air, and in the third or fourth throw it landed with the wheel pretty hard over. It then seems to have jumped 4 or 5 feet according to witnesses, at which time he parted company with the machine and slid between 150 and 175 feet, the machine going on ahead.

"According to marks on the machine it seems to have been travelling most of the time almost upside down, as the greatest wear was on the handle bar more or less on the upper side, the handlebar having been worn nearly through. A careful examination of the machine gives no indication as to why this should have occurred. It had been previously ridden with the front tire too soft, and I told the boys to pump it up. Immediately after this it started on its bad habits. Owing to the fact that the starter has been broken off, and the new one has not come, we have not used it since. The front wheel seems to be perfectly tight, and the adjustment showing absolutely no play whatever, and the head likewise. VanSice has looked it over as well as myself and can give no explanation of this peculiar happening. Examination of the road surface disclosed no visible unevenness which could have started this happening. Fortunately, the boy was not hurt.

"I have been thinking about the use of Allegheny metal. I would suggest looking into this as a possible material for head and tail lamps, tail lamp bracket, saddle bracket, pedals, etc., etc., and cast or bar Allegheny metal for valve covers, oil pump, starter, clutch lever, intake pipe, etc. If it is inexpensive, and I think it must be as it is used in the Ford in place of plated steel, it might be used in place of all plated parts at the present time except cylinders, for Allegheny in combination with stainless steel might do away with plating bills entirely."

# Business Improves

"...General conditions at Indian are very encouraging indeed. Since Alzina and Crocker's visit they are going back visiting dealers and we are receiving telegrams, orders and everything, as a result of their visit. Orders are continuing to come in, so that now any orders received cannot be built until after the 1st of April. This does not include any police business at all.

"The operations in the plant are most satisfactory. We are not losing a single machine and everyone is working smoothly; in fact, everything is 'jake.'

"The last two accounts (Goodyear and Firestone) have now put us on open account terms and the following is a quotation from a letter received from Goodyear:

"'...in view of what we learn we feel that Indian has reached the turning point and that the necessary steps have been taken whereby unprofitable operations are a thing of the past....'

"As a result of Crocker's visit to Chicago we received a wire from the dealer and he wants to put on an extensive campaign immediately on the Dispatch Tow.

"I do not want to be over-enthusiastic but I feel very sure that we are going to do a very nice business this year with the Dispatch Tow.... It is well within possibility that we will manufacture 1,500 of these this year...."

**Indian dealership display, 1931**
The Kansas City Indian shop in 1931. Rollie Free began his lifelong opposition to Harley-Davidson here, in 1923. *Hill/Bentley*

109

**Four, 1932**
The year 1932 ushered in the new look, as seen here on a Four. The Four and Chief got new longer forks, which pushed the steering head higher so that the handlebars were brought farther back toward the rider. This also meant that the favored upright riding posture could be maintained with shorter handlebars that didn't appear so similar to those of a wheelbarrow. The look had first been popularized in the late 1920s by a few British makes, but by 1932 it had become universal. A new front fender was fitted to 1932 Fours and Chiefs. *Hill/Bentley*

*Du Pont Letter to Hosley, March 19, 1931*

# Controls, Scout Generator Noise, Frame Problems

"I notice several things on the new machine which I got which I consider quite serious. I know as well as you do that we cannot interfere with production with changes now. I wish, however, you would look into these matters and see whether you think we can get by with them; in my opinion as (sic) cannot. The first one is that the throw on the brake pedal on the 74 model has been reduced to such an extent that the brake is now not practical. You know what happens when you reduce the throw of a pedal, and this has been done. The throw has been reduced in order that the old pedal can be moved in the forward position, and the oil pump interferes, causing the difficulty. If the offset in the pedal were put farther back everything would be jake.

"The second thing I notice is that there is in the Scout that I have received a frightful noise in the generator drive. From actual tests we find we can hear this five-eights of a mile away. We discovered that the generator drive belt guards was acting like a sound box, and on removing this guard the noise was reduced so that it could be heard only one-eighth of a mile away. As you will realize sound decreases with the square of the distance, this is some reduction in sound. I am told that the noise disappears in about 7,000 miles. I would suggest that you take a few machines at random and observe this noise on the street, or in the yard if you do not wish to get them dirty. The noise is not increased by actually engaging the clutch in gears sohat a good account of it can be obtained by idling the motor.

"Another thing that comes up is that the Duco is still being complained of as being too thin.

"On the new design for 1932, I do not know what was done about the frame where the tubes go into the head. The two tubes running up parallel and bent as in the present Chief and Scout frame are subject to bending. I find that the Wilmington dealers and the Washington dealers both claim that they have never had a sprung frame on a 4, but are getting sprung frames all the time on the Scout and the Chief. What is meant by a "sprung" frame is that after a spill the front wheel will be seen to lean to one side. The tubes running in at an angle as on the four-cylinder machine seem to have absolutely prevented this, and the bending happens to the fork, which is much the best way to have it. I do not remember what was the outcome of our talk on this with Franklin, but I think this should decide us to eliminate the tubes entering the head parallel as they do on the present Chief and Scout, and enter into the head at an angle as on the 4.

"...Please retain this letter to bring to my attention next week, as I wish to talk about the generator drive engineering in the hope of overcoming the noise at this point."

**Scout Pony, 1932**
A new small twin was introduced in the middle of the 1932 sales season. Dubbed the Scout Pony, the 30.50ci, 500cc twins continued in production as the Scout Pony, Junior Scout, and Thirty-Fifty until the end of 1941. *Hill/Bentley*

*Du Pont Letter to Hosley,
October 1, 1931*
## Financial Problems

"I am exceedingly much exercised over the financial situation.... I think there is only one way to combat the situation which will confront us, and that is to begin right now and run the Company almost as it would be run in the hands of a receiver, that is to say, with but one thought in mind—to conserve the cash, remembering all the time what we are to do and the importance of coming out with cash and more cash. I would suggest a program in which we cut out advertising expense, cut out as much experimental expense as possible, cut out as much sales expense as possible, seriously considering canceling our plans for a trip to London and spending no more money on the Property Account than is absolutely necessary to start the new models into production. Despite the additional $50,000 which we hope to get from the sale of the property, the cash outlook does not look good and must be the subject of all our planning...."

*Hosley Letter to du Pont,
November 9, 1931*
## The Thirty-Fifty

"...The little 30.5 model is well along and I expect that within the next day or so we will be able to get photographs and I will mail you a complete set after they are received. Without any doubt, I believe that this is the nicest looking model that Indian has ever built. Everyone is very enthusiastic about it and most everyone has a feeling that they would like to ride it. There may be a little more to the small model than we think as I find that a great many people are afraid of the large model but this little one seems to invite you to ride...."

**Wheels for workers or youths, 1932**
The Scout Pony was Indian's idea of rekindling the once-popular transportation market. Many Scout Pony components were leftover from the defunct Prince single. *Hill/Bentley*

**Scout Pony, 1933**
The Scout Pony got a new front fork in 1933. The small circular housing on the side of the crankcase covered the circuit breaker for the battery ignition. All 1933 Indian twins used this "wasted spark" system, which avoided the use of a distributor by firing both cylinder plugs on each revolution. This was the long-standing Harley-Davidson technique. *Hill/Bentley*

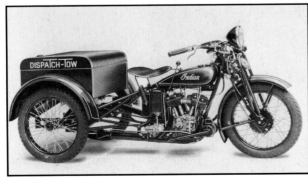

**First Dispatch Tow, 1933**
The first of the nominal 45ci, 750cc Dispatch Tows was this 1933 three-wheeler powered by the Motoplane engine. *Hill/Bentley*

## Hosley Letter to du Pont, January 20, 1932
# Pay Cuts, Layoffs

"...It is now rumored around town that the Union Trust Company is not loaning anything to anyone; in fact, Mr. Fuller informed me that the condition of that bank was such that they could not lend anyone....

"Our vendors have been very fine indeed in extending credit to us, and in practically every case we have been able to obtain the additional time on purchases for the first three months....

"I have spent practically all of the last three days on piece work earnings, day rates, salaries and costs, with the following decision: I have found that piece work earnings are practically the same as they were before we made the original 15% cut and on Monday there is to be another cut of 10% on all piece work and group earnings. Likewise, all day workers such as tool room, service department, parts department, inspection, etc., are to be reduced 10%. I have not made, nor do I contemplate making any reductions in salaried employees. You will recall that every salaried employee has been cut from their original salary approximately 21%, which of course includes the Saturday mornings, although this does not affect their income, and I do not believe that it is either necessary or advisable, as the people who are left are really deserving of raises rather than any further reduction....

"...we have laid off over 30 men in the toolroom, four in the engineering department, three in the order department and some in the service department....

"I was very much interested in the letter from Parke Ross relative to building a motorcycle for Sears Roebuck; however, I would like to withhold sending Parke any details until after I have talked with you about this. The thought I have in mind is to revamp the Prince leaving off the front wheel brake, generator, battery, horn (substituting dry batteries possibly), and every possible accessory, and make this a purely Sears and Roebuck model. This would in no way interfere with our dealer organization; in fact, they would be more than welcome to buy it...."

**Scout, 1933**
This 1933 Scout shows the new generator drive unit that was cast into the primary drive cover instead of bolted on the cover. Chiefs had this feature, too. Introduced in 1932, the Scout was simply a Scout powerplant in a Chief frame. It was not popular with riders who appreciated the lighter and nimbler Model 101. *Hill/Bentley*

*Hosley Letter to du Pont,*
*March 4, 1932*
# Further Cost Cutting

"...I am very much encouraged as the budget as finally laid out balances so that on the sale of 3,500 regular machines and 500 30.50's we should be able to break even on the last three quarters.... This means, however, a great lay-off in our force....

"...In the Racing Department we will have to let Mr. Gustafson go, also quite a lot of the personnel in the Experimental Department. This naturally means curtailed activities and we are going to do a minimum amount of racing and hill climbing this year....

"...Last year we spent $538,000 in the factory and this has now been reduced to $371,000....

Our last year's sales expense was $225,000 and this has been reduced to the rate of $120,000 a year. In doing this it will be necessary to make considerable cutting in our sales force....

"All of this work and turnover is, as you can imagine, rather disagreeable and this afternoon has been appointed the time for notifying all concerned. As I wrote you previously, I felt very keenly the loss for January and this move is the only one possible in order that we go thru this year ending up with sufficient cash at the end to enable us to continue on...."

*Hosley Letter to du Pont,*
*April 29, 1932*
# Four-Day Week

"After you left on Wednesday, I went over several plans with Mr. Wright and Mr. Darrah as to how we could effectively reduce our overhead due to our lack of sales, and it was the opinion—perhaps selfishly—of all of us that we select certain heads of departments who would work five days a week and that the balance of the personnel would go on four days a week.

"Therefore, after careful consideration and analysis, we selected some twelve men who would remain on the five-day week and we have put it into effect starting on Monday. This does not really mean that we are going on four days a week, for the help will alternate days so that the plant will be open a full five days. In the factory, however, they are planning to close down on Wednesday and Saturday, and we will be able to get out our necessary production in four days...."

**Chief, 1933**
For 1933, a new oil pump provided dry-sump
(recirculating) lubrication, as shown on this
Chief. *Hill/Bentley*

**Four, 1933**
The 1933 Fours used a new inlet manifold with
horizontal cooling fins. *Hill/Bentley*

**Armored Car, circa 1933**
An Indian dealer sales kit read: "Armored Car:
Modern criminal practice demands that the
police officer be equipped to cope with the
desperate situations which occasionally arise.
To combat these activities, the police officer
should receive the utmost protection available.
Indian Armored Cars offer this protection: bullet
proof shields of special glass and finest crucible
steel can be folded down when not in use, but are
fitted with loopholes for gun play when needed.
A formidable fortress—to combat the unruly—
to curb mob action—or to perform patrol duty
under dangerous circumstances—yet with all the
mobility of motorcycle equipment." *Indian
dealer sales kit*

*Hosley Letter to du Pont,*
*February 16, 1933*

## Indian Broke!

"...about ten o'clock in the morning I was told by Mr. Darrah that we did not have sufficient monies to meet our payroll. This is the first time that this has ever happened and I therefore went down to the bank and borrowed $10,000 from Mr. Gilbert, which, by the way, he was very nice in lending.

"Our orders have been dropping off continually—so much so that not only did I put into effect the changes which I discussed with you in New York but I also have put the entire office force, including myself, on two-thirds time, and while we are still working five days a week the office hours have been changed to 9:00 to 12:00, and 1:30 to 4:00.... In addition to curtailing the office force, I have closed down the factory completely for one week and this will at least make our payroll condition much better for the future...."

*Hosley Letter to du Pont,*
*February 20, 1933*

## Bankruptcy Considered

"...As I see the picture, we shouldn't even consider a receivership. It would be much better to present the reorganization to the stockholders in the proper manner and I believe that would be able to get sufficient proxies so that the receiver would not be necessary, although of course you could hold this out as a reason for the reorganization. If a receiver were appointed it would be disastrous not only to our creditors but to our customers and I really don't think this will be necessary...."

**Fred Marsh and overhead-valve twin, circa 1933**
Judging from the new look of this speedway bike, and rider Fred Marsh's close connections with the nearby Indian factory, the motorcycle is probably one of the Indian factory specials built to compete with the Crocker overhead-valve Scouts. Other top speedway bikes of the era were the new Crocker overhead-valve single, and English overhead-valve Rudge singles, and Douglas horizontally opposed twins. *Fred Marsh*

**Sport Scout, 1934**
The 1934 45ci Sport Scout replaced the 1933 45ci Motoplane. The keystone frame continued the Prince/Scout Pony/Motoplane setup. At about the same time, British and continental makers were switching from keystone frames. As on earlier Scouts, cylinder head finning was front-to-back, not angled as on later models. *Hill/Bentley*

115

**Chief, 1935**
This 1935 Chief shows new fenders, new nickel-plated cylinders, and new-style optional aluminum cylinder heads. *Hill/Bentley*

**Four, 1935**
Distributor battery ignition was a new option on Fours for 1935. This was the last year for the old Ace-style four-cylinder motor and the first year of the new, deeply rounded and graceful "streamline" fenders. *Hill/Bentley*

# A Flurry of Transcontinental Runs

During Indian's years the transcontinental record was considering by many to be the ultimate test in motorcycling. The first record was made in 1903, in 53 days aboard the predecessor of the Yale motorcycle. From 1906 through 1923, Indian, Ace, and Henderson riders took their turns holding the record. Bad publicity halted these attempts in 1923 with Indian rider Paul Remaly owning the record at 5 3/4 days.

The transcontinental game was renewed in 1935, when Roger and Steve Whiting rode a Chief, double, for about 117 hours for some sort of record. Earl and Dot Robinson answered the challenge with a Harley-Davidson sidecar rig, dropping the time to about 90 hours. In June 1936, Sport Scout rider Rody Rodenburg crossed the continent in 71 hours—or so he claimed. Indian super-fan Rollie Free, although always giving the benefit of the doubt to Indian riders, said Rodenburg cheated by towing the machine for most of the distance, while swapping driving and sleeping time with his buddy. In September, an odd record was set by L. C. Smith. Riding a Chief sidecar rig *solo*, Smith lowered the transcontinental time to about 87 hours. A month later, copilots Bill Connelly and Fred Dauria rode their Harley-Davidson outfit from shore to shore in about 70 hours.

From 1903 through 1934, eight transcontinental records were set, averaging more than three years between each. The sudden interest in the two years 1935 and 1936, produced five records. This marked the end of Indian and Harley-Davidson pursuit of the big record. Overall, Indian claimed seven of the thirteen marks.

**Fred Marsh, 1935**
Rider Fred Marsh is set to leave his Connecticut shop for the 1935 national championship race meet at Syracuse, New York. No car or truck for Marsh, as a sidecar rig was entirely adequate for hauling his racing machine. In fact, Marsh did not buy his first car until more than thirty years later. *Fred Marsh*

**Roger and Steve Whiting, 1935**
In May 1935, Roger and Steve Whiting are greeted in Los Angeles by, right to left, dealer Floyd Clymer, "Long" John O'Conner, former Indian advertising department staffer and current editor of *Motorcyclist*, and Clymer's salesman Morty Graves, one-time Indian board tracker. The brothers had taken turns at the handlebars, jointly piloting the Chief to a new record of 4 days, 20 hours, and 36 minutes. *Hill/Bentley*

**Fred Markwick and Scout, circa 1935**
The late Fred Markwick is about to lose control of this Scout, which has a front fork from a 30.50ci twin. *Fred Markwick collection*

**Indian dealership, circa 1935**
Hard times of the Depression sometimes drove dealers into smaller quarters. In the 1920s, this Kansas City dealership occupied two floors of a new downtown building. *Kinnie/Cox*

**Four, 1935–1936**
The new upside-down Fours were introduced in the summer of 1935. Shown here are members of the Wichita, Kansas, police department. The Dover, Ohio, chief of Police said, "This is the wickedest piece of machinery I have ever had the pleasure of operating... a bundle of dynamite packed into the neatest type of motorcycle ever built... the peppiest and easiest handling outfit we have ever ridden...it is the V-8 of motorcycles for getaway and speed and is the ideal machine for Police work...." *Indian dealer sales kit*

**Sport Scout, 1935**
Beginning in 1935, the Sport Scout was available with optional magneto ignition. The primary drive cover was redesigned to provide an interface section between the primary cover and magneto cover. *Indian dealer sales kit*

**Police Special Chief, 1935**
Indian dealer sales kit reads: "Indian Police Special Chief Motorcycle. Powered by its new Y type heavy duty motor, by far the most popular model for all around utility, is proving its merit in every way as the ideal motorcycle for fast moving, active police organizations." *Indian dealer sales kit*

**Dispatch Tow, 1935**
This is one of those pictures that make you wish you could step into it. To counteract the decade-long slump in sports sales, both Indian and Harley-Davidson pushed sales of commercial machines. The Dispatch Tow was Indian's counter to the Harley-Davidson Servi-Car. *Indian dealer sales kit*

**Dispatch Tow, 1935**
Could this commercial rig, and others like it, be the inspiration for Indian's skirted fender lineup that arrived five years later? According to the sales kit, "One of the innumerable uses which the Indian Dispatch Tow excels is indicated by this installation by a progressive mortician. Leading or convoying safely and without interruption of funerals is found ably done by this sensible unit." *Indian dealer sales kit*

**Chief, 1936**
For 1936, Chiefs, Standard Scouts, and Sport Scouts were fitted with T lines that routed oil from the motor base to the inlet valves. Unfortunately, the new spring covers leaked excessively. The large aluminum cylinder heads made a debut as a 1935 option. Also seen here is the new distributor ignition layout that replaced the Harley-style wasted-spark system. Restoration by Elmer Lower.

**Scout Pony, 1936**
The 1936 Scout Pony was given new streamline fenders and a new muffler and exhaust pipe assembly. The plated pipes and muffler on this publicity model were not standard. Of all the oddities, the little twin crankcase and transmission case were switched from aluminum to iron! *Hill/Bentley*

**Sport Scout, 1935**
The Sport Scout was first officially publicized with Y inlet manifold for the 1936 sales season, but the optional Y manifold was available on 1935 Sport Scouts. This example also has the optional aluminum cylinder heads. *Hill/Bentley*

**Standard Scout, 1936**
A convex headlight lens, large bayonet-style filler caps, and flush-mounted taillight were brought out on 1936 models, as shown on this Standard Scout. *Hill/Bentley*

**Chief, 1936**
The long-standing tandem seat option continued throughout the 1930s, as shown on this 1936 model, but more and more buyers opted for the two-passenger Chum-Me seat (Buddy seat in Harley lingo). Restoration by Elmer Lower.

**Side Van, 1936**
The dealer sales kit reads: "Motorcycle delivery to the public's eye spells a desire on the part of the merchant to provide prompt service to his customers. In addition he prospers by the lowest known operating cost." *Indian dealer sales kit*

**Prince special, 1936**
Fred Marsh's Prince-based speedway "short tracker" bike in 1936. *Fred Marsh*

**Traffic Car, 1936**
"Indian Traffic Cars not only excel in solving light commercial delivery, but provide in addition an unparalleled medium for advertising the merchandise and service of the business house. Many firms invest heavily in this feature with doubly satisfying returns," according to the sales kit. Traffic Cars were powered by the 74ci Chief engine. *Indian dealer sales kit*

**Traffic Car, 1936**
Bodies for Traffic Cars were built by the Waterhouse Company of Webster, Massachusetts. Body features included heavy oak flooring, 20 gauge steel outer shell over oak framework, Tek wood (plywood) roof with canvas outer layer, and mounting by six 7/16in bolts. The total weight of these rigs was 1,100lb. *Indian dealer sales kit*

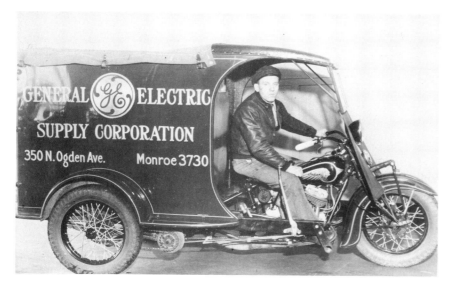

**Traffic Car, 1936**
The sales kit continued: "Indian Traffic Cars are today employed in more than one hundred different kinds of business from the most modest to the world's largest corporations. Its unmatched facilities for quick dependable and economical service invite the interest of every organization having a delivery problem." *Indian dealer sales kit*

# More Street Racing With Rollie Free

Rollie Free continued his street racing in the late 1930s, operating out of his Indian agency in Indianapolis. "We had three or four riders on Sport Scouts in Indianapolis that belonged to our club, the *Indian*apolis club.... We'd go out after club meetings on Wednesday night. Bill Cummins (Indianapolis 500 racer) would come down with his sixty-one Harley that the factory gave him, and we'd all trim 'im. All of 'em—I mean these kids rode flat out, feet out, the whole works, with forty-fives. We had no trouble with Harleys. The sixty-ones weren't fast when they came out; they'd only do about ninety-three or -four miles an hour. A real *good* one would run a hundred and one or two. Hell, the Scouts would run a hundred and ten or twelve miles an hour. I had no trouble.

"I had a boy buy an Indian, who was a Harley rider. His name was Bud Privot. One night at a club meeting he rode up to our door while the meeting was going on, which was held in my store.

"And he says, 'They all trimmed me.' I asked him 'What do mean, they all trimmed you?' 'They ran away from me.' I says, 'Well, what did I promise you when you bought the Scout?' 'You told me seventy-eight miles an hour.' 'Will it do seventy-eight?' He says 'Yes.' 'Then you got what you paid for.'

"I says, 'How fast do you want to go?' He says he wanted to go ninety miles an hour. And I says, 'OK, forty dollars' [Author's note: in 1993-terms, the price was about $800]. He says, 'When can I have it back?' I says, 'Just leave it tonight and pick it up next Wednesday.'

Free visited Maldwyn Jones, former Harley-Davidson factory racer who was now chief motorcycle carburetor engineer for Linkert. Jones advised against a larger venturi but offered the assistance of his timing device. A few days later, Free showed up with the customer's Sport Scout. "'I promised the man ninety miles an hour. You want to ride the Scout?' And he says, 'Yeah.' I sat there and watched him...and heard him go down the road, and it was really running pretty good; sounded real—cackled pretty loud when it got down by me.... He came in and just said. 'It'll do

ninety alright.' That's all he'd say. Well, it would do *over* ninety.

"So at the meeting, here came Bud Privot. He came in swaggering into the store, and another Harley rider with 'im. He says, 'Is the bike ready?' I says, 'Yeah. Just a minute, I'll unlock the shop and roll it out.' He says, 'You want the money?' I says, 'No, go ahead and run it. Ride it first.'

"Well, he disappeared with the Harley rider. Before the meeting closed, about an hour and a half later, he came ridin' up to the front door. He came in and plopped forty dollars on the counter. He said, 'I trimmed all of 'em!' He'd trimmed the whole Harley club.

"...We had no trouble with the local Harley group at all. They wouldn't bet, 'cause they'd lose their money. And I was real cocky; they should've done something about it.

"The factory...sent a fellah at Columbia, Indiana, a stroker job, which they didn't mark on the case of course. He came up to my store in Indianapolis; says 'I'd like to have a match race with you.' I'd tell anybody, 'A hundred bucks, three hundred bucks, what have you got?'

"I says, 'OK, you got a race.' But I says, 'One thing—we measure engines. If yours says sixty-one (1000 cc), it's gotta be sixty-one. And we're gonna run gasoline right out of the pump, or no pay.... He didn't come back. With an honest seventy-four (1200cc) or sixty-one, he couldn't touch me. And they *knew* it.

"I dedicated my life to getting even with these guys [Harley-Davidson].... I did. I mean, I wouldn't put any sand in their engines, but anything I could do to beat 'em was what I would do....

"For fifteen years I never lost a quarter. I offered anybody—I'd bet anybody that would come in my door, and say, 'Well, there's three of 'em sitting there. Which way do you want?' I had a Scout, a Chief, and a four-cylinder that I'd play with. And I'd say, 'You got a hundred bucks, jughead?' That would be my quick remark to them. They would run to the Harley place down there and tell 'em what that so-and-so said up there. But they didn't come down....."

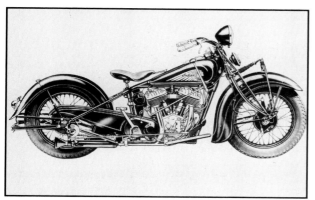

**Chief, 1937**
On the 1937 Chiefs and Standard Scouts, the
new forward-mounted shift lever removed the
delightful direct-action feel imparted by the
1936 and earlier Chiefs and Standard Scouts.
The forward shift lever on the Sport Scouts and
Junior Scouts further degraded shift action,
which had always been indirect on these models.
This photo of a 1937 Chief shows the new
chainguard with more coverage. *Hill/Bentley*

**Ed Kretz, Harrison Reno, Daytona Beach, 1937**
In practice sessions—though others may have
held back—the two fastest machines at the
inaugural Daytona 200 were those of Ed Kretz,
right, and traveling companion Harrison Reno,
left. Kretz won the 200, and Reno was running
third when his motor blew up at 150 miles. The
evening before, both Reno and Kretz had ridden
several drag races up and down the beach on
these machines, for a little money and a lot of
merriment. Perhaps Reno would have finished
the 200, if not for this. *Ed Kretz*

**Daytona 200, 1937**
The year 1937 marked the debut of the Daytona
200, which instantly became the most glamorous
of American races. Presumably, the people
standing on the wet side of the beach are race
officials and pit crew members, but crowd
control was never closely managed at the beach
course. *Clyde Earl*

# A Bet With Rollie Free

"I used to like to go to TT races and things, and if I'd hear a Harley that I know was a stroker, why I'd have 'em protest it. They didn't like me—they hated me. I mean, they had reason to. I really hurt 'em.

"At Louisville, at a race meet, J. B. Jones was riding. And Jones went by an Indian.... And somebody standing by me watching it, said something, and I said, 'Well, either the Indian's sick or the Harley's bigger than it ought to be.' You know, I just made a remark.

"They went over and told Jones. Then the word came over that Jones wanted to see me. So I went over to the pit where Jones and his crew were. He says, 'I understand you thought my motorcycle was stroked.' I said, 'I didn't say that. I said that whenever a Harley went by an Indian it was either oversized or the Indian was sick.'"

To appreciate what follows in this Rollie Free yarn, here's a bit of history. *The J. B. Jones Harley Forty-five racer was the very motorcycle ridden by Joe Petrali to a new Class C (stock) record of 102.047 in January of 1937.*

"And he looked at me. I said, 'Look, I came down here on an Indian Scout, named *Papoose*, with my wife on back.' And I said, 'I can beat the Harley beach record with my wife on back of the machine—double.' He's getting mad—and I want him mad, 'cause that's the only way you can get 'em to bet.

"I said, 'I got three-hundred bucks anytime.' He says, 'I'd like to run a match race.' I says, 'You got it, buddy. Let's see the money.' He says, 'It's a gentlemen's bet.' I said, '*I never had a gentlemen's bet with a Harley guy in my life*. I want the money up.'

"Well, he won't put it up. He didn't have it, I guess. So I said, 'Now look, you said it in front of a bunch of people here. You either race or I'll run you out of Marion, Indiana. I'll make you an ass.' So that ended that. We go home. He doesn't offer any race.

"I sent Rodenburg up, finally, to agitate him. And a hundred bucks was the amount he mentioned. So we went up early in the morning of one day for a two-mile race right out of his town up there, in Marion, with *Papoose*. And hell, it was no race. I mean,

Christ, that thing wouldn't run. Hell, I'm running a hundred ten, twelve, fourteen miles an hour anytime; and he's running a hundred and two if Joe rode it down on the beach. So, you know, how's he gonna beat me? The only way he could beat me would be cheat.

"So we agreed on measurement of engines and gasoline. Everything was agreed this way. And that's the way it would have been, brother, 'cause if he won, I wanted to know *how*. There was only one way brother; it had to be big, or nitro, or something of that nature in it. And I made sure that he didn't get any nitro in it while I was there watching anyway, 'cause we emptied tanks, drained 'em, flushed carburetors and everything. But, we had no trouble (beating Harleys). So I did win a hundred bucks.

"And he made a remark—we're measuring the engines in front of the Marion shop. And he pulled one head off. And Walt Pearson who used to work for Crocker taught me something years ago, when they make us measure an Indian. Walt would take a couple of rags, slide 'em under the cylinder head when he's ready to lift it; one went over the valve—he'd hold his hand over it—and the other one with the head, and he'd put the head down and sit on it so you couldn't see the shape of the head. And he'd have his hand over the valve, and all you could see was the bore and stroke, which is all you're allowed to measure. There wasn't anything different about it; it was so stock it would've killed 'em. But it made it more of a mystery out of it. So they all went [away, thinking] 'I wonder what the head looks like. I wonder what the hell....'

"While he's in my trailer, we're gonna measure it [Free's Scout]. He says, 'I've got an eighty' [1300 cc], he says, 'I'd like to run.' I says, 'Well, I'll tell what I'll do. I've got a Chief that runs pretty good too. But I won't even use the Chief; I'll just run the Scout. You want to bring your Eighty out now?'

"He didn't! Brother, they didn't! I could trim his damn eighty with the Scout, for Christ's sake. What are you talking about, man, they're just a bunch of talkers."

**Joe Hosley and Ed Kretz, 1937**
Indian General Manager Joe Hosley congratulates Ed Kretz for his victory in the inaugural Daytona 200. Hosley had been E. Paul Du Pont's manager at Du Pont Motors prior to running Indian, and he enjoyed Du Pont's complete confidence. Du Pont's money and Hosley's leadership kept Indian alive during the Great Depression. *Ed Kretz*

**Sport Scouts, 1938**
This is one of a series of photos used in the 1938 sales catalogs, *Indian News*, and various advertisements. In the foreground handling the stopwatch is Bud Acker, factory advertising manager. Holding the checkered flag is Fritzie Baer, proprietor of the Spingfield Indian dealership located in the factory basement. The riders are the Castonguay brothers, Frenchie and Woodsie. *Hill/Bentley*

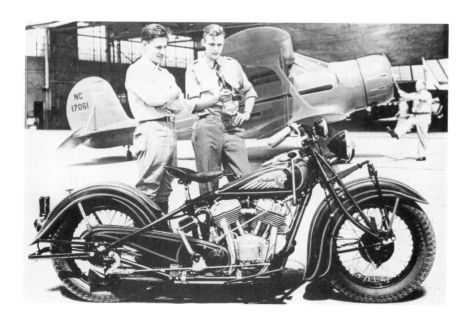

**Chief, 1938**
Another of the 1938 publicity photos shows Bud Acker, left, and friend admiring the Chief. In the background, a man starts a classic Stagger Wing Beech. *Hill/Bentley*

**Junior Scout, 1938**
The 1938 Junior Scout was given minor updates
such as a new horn. Restoration by Elmer Lower.

**Police Special Chief, 1938**
Indian advertising claimed, "The Indian Police
Special 74 is by far the most popular Twin
cylinder motorcycle in America and has proved
its merit in every way. Used exclusively by such
departments as Massachusetts State Police,
New York City, Illinois State Police, North
Carolina Highway Patrol, Battle Creek, Michigan,
and a host of other departments both large and
small." *Indian dealer sales kit*

**Instrument panel, 1938**
One of the hallmark features of the 1938 models
was the new instrument panel. This panel shape
continued through 1947 but the gray switch, and
red and gray speedometer and ammeter, were
unique to 1938. *Indian dealer sales kit*

*Right*
**Rollie Free, Daytona Beach, 1938**
In March 1938, Rollie Free and crew arrived at
Daytona Beach for a crack at the American Class
C (stock motorcycles) records for 74ci, 1200cc
and 45ci, 750 cc records. Free had vowed to
break Harley-Davidson's 45ci record by 10mph,
or he wouldn't come home. *Hill/Bentley*

**Rollie Free, Daytona Beach, 1938**
Class C was relatively new, having been
launched in 1933, and not much emphasis had
been given earlier to Class C records in as much
as Class C was supposed to be a nonprofessional
game. Harley-Davidson owned the 45ci mark at a
mere 102.048mph, an afterthought in Harley's
Daytona Beach Class A (unrestricted) record runs
the previous year. Here, Free, on the Sport Scout,
demonstrates his prone style later made famous
with his postwar Vincent runs in a bathing suit.
*Rollie Free*

**E. C. Smith and Rollie Free,
Daytona Beach, 1938**
AMA executive secretary and racing boss
E. C. Smith congratulates Free after his run of
111.55mph, which gave Indian a 9.502mph
margin over the old Harley-Davidson record.
Free went home anyway, despite being 0.498mph
short of his vow—he was handicapped by a side
wind, he explained. Note the bottle in Smith's
hip pocket; the advertising department would
later diplomatically airbrush the liquor bottle
away. *Emmett Moore collection*

**Rollie Free, Daytona Beach, 1938**
On the Chief, Free ran a couple of miles per hour
slower than on the Sport Scout, due to excessive
oil buildup in the crankcase, or wet sumping as it
was called. Still, the 109.65mph was a Class C
record. *Hill/Bentley*

**Hap Alzina and "Arrow"
streamliner fairing, 1938**
In 1938, West Coast distributor Hap Alzina set
his eyes and wallet on bigger stuff than Class C
records. He commissioned the design and
fabrication of a streamliner capable of bettering
the international record of 173mph held by
German Ernst Henne on a BMW streamliner.
*Hill/Bentley*

**"Arrow" streamliner, 1938**
The Arrow streamliner was powered by a 61ci,
1000cc variant of the 1926 45ci, 750cc racers.
The frame was one of the old Powerplus Daytona
jobs. *Sam Pierce collection*

*Right*
**"Arrow" streamliner, 1938**
Red Fenwick, rider Fred Ludlow, and Hap Alzina
look over the naked Arrow motorcycle. All on-site
photos in this series were taken during the course
of secret testing at Muroc Dry Lake. On the trailer
behind the three musketeers, covered in canvas,
were the sections of the streamliner shell. Alzina
didn't want any publicity prior to a planned trip
to the Bonneville salt flats for the official speed
runs. Muroc, about 125 miles from Los Angeles,
is now called Rogers Dry Lake and is the site of
the present-day Edwards Air Force Base, scene of
numerous space shuttle landings. *Hill/Bentley*

**"Arrow" streamliner, 1938**
The summer heat bounces up off Muroc Dry Lake, where temperatures well above 100 degrees Fahrenheit are common. Throughout the day, preparations continue. *Hill/Bentley*

**"Arrow" streamliner, 1938**
As dusk arrives, the temperature drops sharply into the low 80s. During the high desert night, the thermometer will fall farther to the refreshing 60s. The naked motorcycle has been prepared, but the streamliner shell sections were still packed away in secretive canvas. *Hill/Bentley*

**"Arrow" streamliner, 1938**
The next morning, Fenwick finishes securing the front section to the bike, then makes some adjustment, or perhaps just pretends to do so for the photographer. *Hill/Bentley*

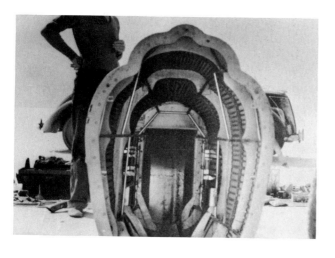

**"Arrow" streamliner fairing, 1938**
The rear section of the streamliner shell was
nearly ready to be moved forward and secured to
the front section. *Hill/Bentley*

**"Arrow" streamliner, 1938**
A smiling Alzina helps Fenwick and others
secure the two halves of the streamliner shell.
Inside, Ludlow probably wasn't smiling, as
there was no provision for escape in event of
an emergency. All Muroc tests were successful,
and the team left confident that their upcoming
Bonneville runs in September would bring
Indian international recognition. However, at
Bonneville Ludlow was unable to control the
streamliner at about 145mph, and the streamliner
was parked, never to run again. The Alzina crew
did manage to set new Class (stock) records of
115.126mph and 120.747mph on the Sport Scout
and Chief, respectively. *Hill/Bentley*

133

**Chief, circa 1938**
A day in the life of a Southern California dry lake. This was a Chief prepared by Frank Chase and Max Bubeck, and due to the latter's smaller frame, ridden by Bubeck in many speed trials. *Max Bubeck*

**Horseplay, circa 1938**
Indians are classics today, but in their day they were just motorcycles meant to be ridden hard and to withstand the abuse of horseplay like this. On the Four is Max Bubeck. *Max Bubeck*

**1300cc trail bike, circa 1938**
In the Indian-versus-Harley days, bigger meant better in every respect. The bigger the motorcycle, the better it was for both touring and off-road riding. Here, Bubeck and buddies maneuver his 1936 Four across a gully. Bubeck updated his Four with the 1937 twin-carburetor setup. *Max Bubeck*

**Model 741, 1939**
Although known as the Model 741, the military light twin was designed in 1939. Displacement was 30.5ci, 500cc to comply with military procurement specifications that Indian erroneously thought would also be imposed by the US military. Competitive testing in 1939 resulted in the selection of the Harley-Davidson Forty-Five as the standard US military motorcycle. Nevertheless, substantial sales of the Model 741 were made to British, Canadian, and other Allied forces. *Ian Campbell*

**Four, 1939**
Magneto ignition became available again on the 1939 Four, after a one-year absence as an option. Restoration by Pete Bollenbach. *John O. L. Finucan*

**Four, 1939**
Classic Four lines are evident from this angle. The paint scheme was the same optional V-panel available from 1935, but a new World's Fair paint scheme was available in 1939. *Finucan*

**Sport Scout, 1939**
This 1939 Sport Scout shows the new muffler and upswept chrome tailpipe that were features of both the Sport Scout and the Chief. The World's Fair paint scheme joined the long-running V-panel as one of the two available paint stylings for two-color finishes. World's Fair or V-panel striping patterns were also options on the one-color finishes. *Hill/Bentley*

**Jimmy Kelly, circa 1939**
Jimmy Kelly looks over Jimmy Hill's Sport Scout equipped with special close-finned aluminum cylinder heads. The year was 1939 or later, which can be verified by the World's Fair paint scheme on the Sport Scout in the background. The scene: Daytona Beach. Kelly was sponsored by Los Angeles dealer Floyd Clymer. *Ed Kretz*

**Al Chasteen and Chet Billings, 1939**
On August 6, 1939, Al Chasteen accepts a trophy from *Motorcyclist* editor and AMA referee Chet Billings, for winning the ten-mile trophy dash. The trophy dash events of the era featured the day's fastest time trial qualifiers. The four fastest qualifiers for the important Oakland 200-mile national championship, rode Indians. But Harley-Davidson star Jack Cottrell won the championship. Thus continued the tradition of Milwaukee winning most of the long events where speed took a back seat to reliability, and Springfield winning most of the shorter events and time trials where speed was paramount. *Ed Kretz*

**Daytona Beach, 1939**

After Indian won the first Daytona, it didn't get any more prewar Daytona 200 titles. Harley-Davidson rider Benny Campanale won the 1939 and 1940 Daytona 200s, and Canadian Norton ace Billy Mathews won in 1941. Out for a leisurely putt at the 1939 Daytona race meet were, left to right: Frenchy Castonguay, Ed Kretz, Jimmy Kelly, and Woodsie Castonguay. Both of the Castonguays were using the factory accessory racing windscreen. You can almost feel the same wind in your face and smell the same air. *Ed Kretz*

# Daytona Beach In The Prewar Years

Of the prewar Daytona Beach scene, Indian staffer Matt Keevers said: "Races like Daytona back in the thirties were so much fun; we had so many privileges. Race week when they were on the beach, we'd usually be over on Route A over on the other side of the mainland, you might say. There used to be a couple of places with maybe fifteen- or twenty-one-car garages out in back. And they'd be full. Each one would have somebody in there with a motorcycle from some part of the country. There were several places where we'd go, and beach time would be open for a couple of hours, depending on the tide. You'd just warm your motorcycle up, and just, say on Tuesday—you had four or five days yet before the race—and you'd just ride it down the street, right downtown and over onto the beach and go out and run, you know. You can't do those things much now these days, but it certainly was a wonderful situation. The police just never paid any attention to you. Racers would be going down the streets with the straight pipes and everything, and the police didn't bother you at all, as long as you had a number on it. It was a *real* kind of thing, and it was easy to get *close* to, to *feel* the kind of excitement."

**Daytona Beach, circa 1939**
Since Daytona Beach was such a large part of Class C racing glory, we'll pause for a few photos that are representative of the beach races—the exact years aren't important, in other words. The rider on the number 132 Sport Scout is Albert "Whitey" Westerberg of Springfield, Massachusetts. He wears the jacket of Baton Rouge dealer Gonzales. Indian always had its pockets of above-average success, and Baton Rouge was one of them. This appears to be the south turn at the end of the asphalt (tarmac) road behind the beach. *Clyde Earl*

**Daytona Beach, circa 1939**
The north turn at Daytona Beach began in deep, dry sand, then the sand feathered on to the asphalt back straight. So, you could fall down for either of two reasons: uncontrolled wobbling in the deep stuff, or a sudden bit of traction after sliding along the sand-covered pavement. *Hill/Bentley*

**Daytona Beach, circa 1939**
Action coming out of the north turn onto the asphalt road. Rider number 111 was sliding smoothly over the pavement heavily "salted" with sand. When the sand coating thinned out, the front wheel suddenly grabbed traction and quit sliding, but the rear wheel continued to slide out.
*Hill/Bentley*

**American TT race, circa 1939**
A Chief rider takes a spill in a so-called TT race. Originally called miniature TTs, after *the* Isle of Man TT race, the American TTs were popular because they offered racing on the biggest bikes, showed dirt racing with brakes, and were much easier courses to lay out than the deceptively simple looking flat tracks that were an old staple. The layout ease was especially important because much professional racing was promoted by local motorcycle clubs using volunteer labor.
*Hill/Bentley*

140

**Woodsie Castonguay**
Woodsie Castonguay shows off the style that made him and brother Frenchie among the top racers of the late-1930s and 1940s. *Emmett Moore*

*Below*
**Ed Kretz, circa 1939**
Ed Kretz prepares to do battle on a 1939 Sport Scout. Kretz is revving his motor, as indicated by the plugged ears of the man behind. Loud! *Kretz*

*Chapter 6*

# 1940–1947
## *The Baton is Twice Passed*

The du Pont-Hosley team ended in February 1940 when Joe Hosley died of a heart attack. After Hosley's death, E. Paul du Pont never seemed to regain the enthusiasm he had once felt for Indian.

The 1940 lineup introduced the famous skirted fenders that are the most prominent feature of the later Indians. Plunger rear suspension also made its debut on the 1940 Chief and Four and a year later on the Sport Scout.

**Model 841, 1940**
The Model 841 45ci, 750cc shaft-drive motorcycle was based on a motor earlier designed for a non-motorcycle application for the Air Corps and Navy. Development of the 841 began in 1940, and the first prototype probably entered testing before the year was out. This was Indian's first foot-shift motorcycle. *Indian archives photo copied by George Hays*

With most of the world already at war, Indian enjoyed booming business due to both military sales and the restless civilian populace that sensed that the days of peace in the United States were coming to an end. Indian's 1940 production totaled 10,431 machines, which included 5,000 Chiefs built for the French Army. This was as close as the post-1926 Indian company ever came to matching Harley-Davidson, which sold 10,855 units, almost all civilian models. In 1941, Indian built 8,739 motorcycles compared to Harley-Davidson's 18,428. Indian's profits soared to $703,000 in 1940, and remained respectable at $381,000 in 1941.

Military production took over at Indian in 1942, with only a dribble of civilian 1942 models produced in late 1941 and early 1942. Indian produced 16,647 machines in 1942 and 16,456 in 1943, and earned profits of $1.1 million and $400,000, respectively. Motorcycle production plummeted to 3,881 in 1944 and 2,070 in 1945. Nonmotorcycle defense work helped matters, but losses in 1944 and 1945 totaled $700,000 and $600,000, respectively.

The past fifteen years (excludes 1930 with no available data) under du Pont management now totaled a cumulative production of 91,052 Indians compared to similar production of over 196,000 Harley-Davidsons during the same period. Cumulative du Pont era losses totaled

$260,000. Tired of the financial roller-coaster ride, du Pont sought a buyer for the Indian Motocycle Company.

After a false start with an outfit called Lawrance Aeronautical, in November 1945, E. Paul du Pont and his brother Francis sold their controlling interests to a group headed by Ralph B. Rogers. Rogers' aim was to build a line of lightweight European-style motorcycles that he was convinced would sell in large numbers.

The 1946 Indian lineup included only the Chief, which was updated with a new hydraulically damped girder fork derived from the military shaft-drive Model 841. Chief production totaled 3,621, compared to Harley-Davidson's total of 15,554. Production was continually hampered by supplier problems concerning castings and heat treating, which caused many items to fail Indian's quality-control inspections. Engineering efforts continued on a planned postwar Sport Scout, which was to be equipped with the Chief front fork, rear generator drive like the Chief, and modified Chief rear suspension.

Rogers purchased the Torque Manufacturing Company of Plainfield, Connecticut. The Torque company had employed G. Briggs Weaver, former chief engineer at Indian, to design a line of modular motorcycles including a 220cc single, a 440cc vertical twin, and an 880cc inline four.

In 1947, Rogers secured additional financing for his expansion plans, at the cost of drawing into the management loop the Atlas Corporation, the Chemical Bank, and the Marine Midland Bank. Shortly afterward, Rogers announced that the historic Indian factory on State Street was for sale. He then merged his other companies with Indian. Production of 1947 Chiefs totaled 11,849, compared to Harley-Davidson's total of more than 20,000.

Racing prestige was enhanced by Johnny Spiegelhoff's win of the 1947 Daytona 200 on a prewar Sport Scout. While long-time Indian fans

**Mrs. Clem Murdaugh and Sport Scout, 1940**
Mrs. Clem Murdaugh of West Chester, Pennsylvania, shows us her 1940 Sport Scout with streamlined saddlebags. Her husband Clem was an active competition rider. The Sport Scout combination of skirted fenders and rigid frame were unique to 1940. *Hill/Bentley*

hoped for a resumption of Sport Scout production, problems at the factory were making this less and less likely.

By the end of 1947, Indian president Ralph B. Rogers looked ahead with optimism. In the words of staffer Matt Keevers, Rogers could sell ice to Eskimos. The enthusiasm was contagious and it seemed that Indian was on the verge of another great era, sparked by another model called the Scout, the forthcoming vertical twin designed by G. Briggs Weaver.

**Model 841, 1940**
The Model 841 front fork was the basis of the fork used on the 1946 through 1948 Chief; the Chief's fork was longer and narrower, however. *George Hays*

**Indian ad, 1941**
An Indian advertisement in *Public Safety*. *Indian dealer sales kit*

## DIES SUDDENLY
### *Motorcycle Industry Mourns Loss of Loring F. Hosley*

The motorcycle industry mourns the loss of one of its best beloved and most important personages in the death of Loring F. Hosley, vice president and general manager of the Indian Motocycle Company. He passed away at his home in Southwick, Mass., February 28 following a heart attack.... Only 48 years of age, it was his guiding hand that had helped the motorcycling sport regain and increase its popularity during the last decade.... [H]e came to Indian in 1930 from Wilmington, Delaware, where he had been general manager of the Du Pont Motors Company...."

Du Pont appointed twenty-three-year Indian veteran Dwight L. Moody as the new Vice-President and General Manager. Moody's background was in purchasing.

*From* Indian News, *March 1940*

**Thirty-Fifty, Model 540, 1940**
The 30.50ci twin was renamed the Thirty-Fifty for the 1940 season. Skirted fenders, a new front fork, tanks the same size as the larger models, and compression saddle springs were all new features. *Indian dealer sales kit*

**Four and sidecar, 1940**
The newly styled 1940 sidecar was a must to keep styling consistent with the new skirted fender motorcycles. *Indian dealer sales kit*

**Dispatch Car, 1940**
The 1940 Indian Dispatch Car with standard body was designed for service station use in delivery of customer cars and for small parts or package delivery. *Indian dealer sales kit*

**Dispatch Car, 1940**
The 1940 Indian Dispatch Car, with optional large body, handled bigger chores. *Indian dealer sales kit*

**Side Van, 1940**
Two versions of the Side Van
Commercial Indian motorcycle
were offered, the closed body
shown here and an open body.
*Indian dealer sales kit*

**Police Special Seventy-Four,
1940**
The 1940 Police Special Indian
Seventy Four advertisement had
the following caption: "Twin
cylinder heavy duty motorcycle
with patented Indian dry sump
lubrication, spring frame, triple
stem fork—available with either
5.00x16 or 4.00x18 tires and
wheels. Controls may be
reversed at no extra cost. Radio
equipment extra." *Indian dealer
sales kit*

**Police Special Four, 1940**
The 1940 Police Special Four
remained popular with police
departments due to its easy
starting. *Indian dealer sales kit*

**Police riders, 1940**
This Connecticut police department was split between Chiefs and Fours, but local dealer Fred Marsh was happy either way. *Fred Marsh*

*Left*
**Joe Duke, Langhorne, Pennsylvania, 1940**
A typical prewar Sport Scout flat tracker, seen at the 1940 Langhorne, Pennsylvania, race meet. The rider is Joe Duke. Langhorne was a one-mile steeply banked egg-shaped dirt track, oiled and hard packed until the surface was almost like asphalt. Long and steeply banked dirt tracks were called speedways in the United States. *Hill/Bentley*

**101 Scout and Chief, circa 1940**
The charm of the 101 Scout, its handling, is suggested here when compared to a much more ponderous Chief. As used machines years past their production life, the 101 Scouts could be bought cheap, which further added to their popularity as competition conversions. On the left, Abe Christopherson; on the right, Harlen "Hob" Krause; both of Beloit, Wisconsin. *Hill/Bentley*

**101 Scout, the poor man's racer, circa 1940**
In the late 1930s, 1940, and 1941, a few racers soldiered on with the 101 Scouts, usually outfitted with Sport Scout cylinders and heads.
*Hill/Bentley*

**101 Scout, circa 1040**
The 101 didn't have the "modern" look of the later Indians, but its lines have endured the test of time. The late Sport Scout cylinders and heads seem right at home. Abe Christopherson, again.
*Hill/Bentley*

# SMOOTH RIDING... POWER

Indian Spring Frame gives you the matchless combination of fast-driving power and flight-smooth riding in a motorcycle unequalled for crack smartness.

No matter how rough the road, the riding's smooth on an Indian Spring Frame "Police Special" . . . better control, greater safety and less fatigue for the man in the saddle. Ask your local Indian dealer to let you road test this superb machine . . . see why so many police departments are mounting their men on Indian Spring Frame Motorcycles.

## INDIAN MOTOCYCLE CO.
*Springfield, Mass.*

## 40 Years Pride of the Force

*Indian* DOUBLE ACTION SPRING FRAME

SPEED! CONTROL! ACTION!

ONLY INDIAN
HAS THE MIRACLE

## SPRING FRAME

It's new, *sensational!*
Spring Frame floats you
over the roughest roads
as though they were
smooth concrete — gets
you there and gets action
*fast!* Your Indian grips
the road, under perfect
control. You get away
faster, brake better.
Spring Frame, brilliant
new styling, and many
other features make the
1940 Indians the world's
outstanding police motor-
cycles. Ask your Indian
dealer or write Dept. PS4.

**INDIAN MOTOCYCLE CO.**
*Springfield, Mass.*

MORE THAN
EVER
the PRIDE
OF THE FORCE

*Indian*

## SPRING FRAME

New, coil-type, pressure lubricated
spring frame combined with knee-
action fork and velvet action seat
gives you the world's smoothest
motorcycle ride, no matter how
rough the road.

# Indian Racing 1933–1941

A new "stock" motorcycle game made its debut in 1933, partly because Indian and Harley-Davidson were too strapped to continue supporting Class A and B professional racing. Class C gathered momentum from 1933 through 1937, and by 1938 had eclipsed the old Class A game in spectator support. The two American factories also gradually renewed their racing support, although camouflaging this under the pretense of rider ownership and factory noninvolvement, as required by Class C rules.

In Class C, Indian fared better than Harley-Davidson during the prewar era. The historic Scout bore-stroke combination, porting development assisted by the famed Massachusetts Institute of Technology, and magneto ignition all benefited Indian. In describing this era and his builder/tuner who became a legend, former Harley-Davidson star Sam Arena said that Tom Sifton made his name by building Harley-Davidsons that would run *as fast as* (not faster than!) Indians.

Big Indian wins included the 1936 Savannah 200 and Langhorne 100, the 1937 (inaugural) Daytona 200 and Langhorne 100, the 1938 Langhorne 100 and Laconia 200, and the 1939 through 1941 Langhorne 100s, with Ed Kretz winning three of the Langhorne bouts. Indian riders won the Springfield, Illinois, 25-mile national every year from 1937 through 1941, and in accord with the custom were awarded the prestigious Number One plate for these victories. In 1938, Indian held every Class C half-mile dirt-track record. In 1939, Indian riders owned eleven of fourteen Class C records, including all half-mile marks and four out of six mile-track marks.

In 1941, Harley-Davidson brought out the WR, their first out-of-the-box Class C racer, signalling tougher going ahead for Indian. Still, at the end of 1941 Indian owned its fifth consecutive Number One Plate, the 100-mile Laconia and Langhorne titles, the Oakland 200-mile title, and nine of fourteen Class C records.

**Sport Scout, circa 1940**
Class C rules permitted swapping the original manufacturer's parts between various models. Junior Scout forks and tanks were popular Sport Scout alterations for racing. *Hill/Bentley*

*Previous pages*
**Indian ads, 1941**
Typical Indian advertisements in *Public Safety* magazine. *Indian dealer sales kit*

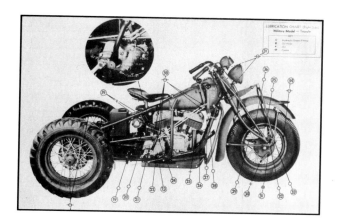

**Military tricycle, 1941**
In December 1941, both Indian and Harley-Davidson delivered prototype three-wheelers to the Army for testing. The two companies, of course, could not suspect that the four-wheel Jeep would soon relegate motorcycles to a much less important status than they had during World War I. Harley-Davidson records show that its trike got low marks for handling; Indian's probably got the same poor grades. Indian's trike used a Chief motor, and Harley-Davidson's used a derivative of their 61ci overhead-valve twin. *Jimmy Hill*

**Model M1, circa 1942**
During World War II Indian designed this Model M1, termed the Extra Light Solo. The side-valve motor had a bore and stroke of 2 1/2x2 3/4in, for a displacement of 13.50ci, 221cc. The generator drive cover suggests belt drive was used. *Hill/Bentley*

**Model M1, circa 1942**
The primary drive and engine dimensions suggest the M1 was the forerunner of the postwar Arrow lightweights; however, the double-tube frame was not carried over into the postwar models. The rear brake was heel actuated. *Hill/Bentley*

**Model M1, circa 1942**
Indian staffer Walt Brown demonstrates the light
weight of the Model M1. The M1 was intended
to be airdropped in a crate. Testing at Indian
consisted of dropping a crated M1 from one of
the upper floors to ground level. *Hill/Bentley*

**Military Scout, 1943**
Indian featured the Model 741 and the 45ci
Model 642B continually in *Indian News*, but
US forces didn't use them except for a few in
standby status as part of the Lend-Lease program.
*Indian News*

**Model X44, circa 1944**
The Indian Motocycle Company's last complete
design was this inline four. The Model X44 was
first tested in either 1944 or 1945. The frame
was from the Model 841 shaft-drive twin, as
were the tank and top instrument panel. The
tank was modified to include a dummy section
that housed the air cleaner. As shown, the
configuration was circa 1950, based on the front
fender. Owner Clinton Feld looks justifiably
proud. *Emmett Moore collection*

**Model X44, circa 1944**
A glass plate was installed over the driveshaft housing to permit engineering studies. All valves were upstairs, and the inlet manifold can be seen exiting into the dummy tank section housing the air cleaner. *Emmett Moore collection*

**Model X44, circa 1944**
The crankcase was of barrel layout, so the crankshaft had to be "threaded" into position with the lower engine cover removed. Two cylinders exhausted from each side, permitting a symmetrical exhaust layout. *Emmett Moore collection*

**Vaughn Monroe at Indian factory, 1944**
In December 1944, famous band leader and singer Vaughn Monroe, right, visited the Indian factory. Here, he observes a Service School class in progress under the direction of Erle "Red" Armstrong, who had lately taken on a new nickname, "Pop." *Hill/Bentley*

**Vaughn Monroe, 1944**
While at the Indian factory, Monroe took a spin on this machine prepared for the New Brunswick, Canada, police department. Monroe's mount was a typical wartime version of the Chief. *Hill/Bentley*

**Vaughn Monroe, 1944**
Come now, things couldn't have been all that complicated, could they? Indian staffer Carl White points out features. Monroe was a genuine enthusiast, or he wouldn't have saddled up in the New England winter. *Hill/Bentley*

**Model 741s, circa 1944**
Few Model 741 motorcycles saw combat duty and none of them fought in US colors. This group of Model 741 motorcycles was unloaded for use by the expatriate Polish Army, according to information provided by the USSR. The Soviets had earlier used Model 741 machines.
*Hill/Bentley*

157

# Du Pont Courts Buyer; Leads to Rogers Purchase

In April 1945, arrangements were made with the Lawrance Aeronautical Corporation of Linden, New Jersey, so that key Lawrance managers and engineers were jointly employed and paid by the two companies. That was the proclaimed theory, but the announcement to Indian stockholders added that Indian was paying all the salaries of the effected Lawrance people. Indian proposed to add 100,000 shares of stock, and Lawrance was granted the right to purchase up to 126,854 shares of Indian stock up to

March 15, 1950. Lawrance was a builder of auxiliary aircraft engines and instruments, and du Pont's message to the stockholders stated that the anticipated merger would benefit both companies. Du Pont assumed the title of Chairman of the Board and turned over the office of Indian President to Lawrance president Roland Burnstan.

On October 24, 1945, Lawrance exercised their option and sold their stock to Ralph Rogers and the Atlas Corp. of New York.

**Chief, Model 344, circa 1944**
Police and civilian versions of the military Model 344 Chief were produced in limited numbers during the war for essential defense and municipal use. The homely fenders were in response to the government's opposition to skirted fenders because of the unnecessary use of metal. The officer was Arnold LeTendre of the Springfield police department. *Hill/Bentley*

**Hap Jones birthday party, 1945**
Successful dealers were
good promoters and prewar
motorcycling was dominated by
organized activities. These three
riders pose at the annual Hap
Jones birthday party held in the
rolling rural hills of Northern
California. Their mounts
symbolize the dominance of
Indian and Harley-Davidson, but
with the growing awareness of
British motorcycles such as this
Triumph. *Hap Jones collection*

**Vertical twin prototype, circa 1945**
For the Torque Engineering Company of
Plainfield, Connecticut, former Indian chief
engineer G. Briggs Weaver designed this twin and
a companion single and four that shared major

engine components. The original layouts called
for 10.5, 21, and 42ci (175, 350, and 700cc). In
the summer of 1945, new Indian president Ralph
Rogers purchased the Torque company. *Emmett
Moore collection*

**Indian factory, 1946**
Indian president Ralph Rogers was convinced
that a new one-story plant was essential to
large-scale modern production of the proposed
Torque machines. In September 1946, Indian
bought from the federal government this factory
complex in east Springfield. The buildings had
been owned by Indian in the World War I years,
and during World War II had been used to build
Rolls-Royce aircraft engines. *Bob Finn*

**Jimmy Hill and vertical twin prototype,
circa 1946**
Long-time factory staffer Jimmy Hill took the
prototype twin on a day-long outing, and with
typical test rider technique, managed to inflict
major damage on the machine. After getting the

prototype to limp home, he wrote a scathing test
report detailing every failure. Hill's report was
buried by middle management, and Hill had
nothing more to do with testing of the prototype.
*Jimmy Hill*

160

**Vertical twin prototype, circa 1946**
During 1946, the prototype vertical twin was fitted with telescopic front forks. Prototype cylinder heads differed from production models. The prototype had angled mating surfaces for the valve covers; the production models had a horizontal mating surface. The exposure of the oil line to the cylinder head was eliminated by routing the oil line to the cylinder head through holes in the cylinder cooling fins. *Hill/Bentley*

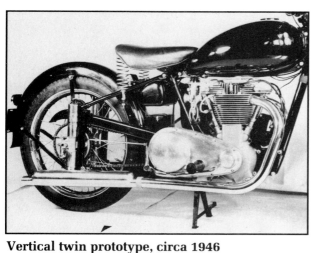

**Vertical twin prototype, circa 1946**
The tank with centrally located filler cap gave way to the production tank with dummy twin-cap appearance. On the production models, the simulated second cap was a built-in ignition switch. Other production changes were a new saddle and new exhaust pipes. At some point the displacements of the modular twins and singles were increased to 26.6 and 13.3ci (436 and 218cc), respectively. These 25 percent increases may have contributed to the poor reliability record of the later production models. *Hill/Bentley*

**Vertical twin prototype, circa 1946**
The underside of the prototype vertical twin shows another major change forthcoming on the production models. The prototype frame was the keystone type, with the lower rear section connected to an engine plate. Production models used a cradle frame, with the lower rear horizontal tubes carried forward under the engine to join the front down tube. *Hill/Bentley*

**Torque four prototype, circa 1946**
This is the four-cylinder Torque design, which shared major engine components with the single and twin. *Emmett Moore collection*

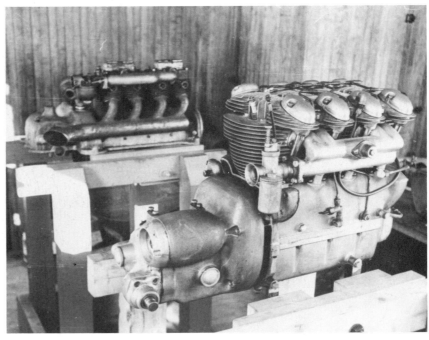

**Torque four prototype, circa 1946**
The Torque modular concept was a good idea, as was in evidence in this workbench photo. At the time this photo was taken, the Torque four was owned by Henry Wing, Sr., cofounder of the Antique Motorcycle Club of America. *Woody Carson*

162

**Chief, 1946**
The 1946 Chief continued the long tradition of Indian police business. *Jimmy Hill*

**Chief, 1946**
For 1946, the Chief got girder-by-coil forks derived from the Model 841, and an Indian-head tank emblem. This is a typical full dresser. *Jimmy Hill*

**Ernie Roccio and Sport Scout, circa 1946**
The postwar racing scene saw the influx of British motorcycles, of which the earliest in large numbers were Triumphs. The Sport Scout rider is Ernie Roccio. *Clyde Earl*

**Ralph Rogers, G. Briggs Weaver and Chief, 1947**
Indian president Ralph Rogers, left, and Chief engineer G. Briggs Weaver, right, pose with a 1947 Chief in the office area of the old Wigwam. The Chief was the only Indian model produced and sold during the 1947 sales season. *Clyde Earl*

**Indian riders, 1947**
The gang shows off typical 1947 motorcycling attire and Indian accessories. Left to right, they are: Bob Finn, Matt Keevers, Bobby Baer, Butch Baer, and J. R. Kelly. *Bob Finn*

**Max Bubeck and Four, 1947**
Max Bubeck won the 500-mile Greenhorn Enduro, a grueling Southern California grind that took riders from scorching desert to chilly mountains and back. His 1939 Four was equipped with telescopic forks manufactured by the Vard company of Pasadena, California. *Max Bubeck*

**Bill Meador and Chief, 1947**
By 1947, the Chief was on its last leg as a racer. The rider was Bill Meador who had just won the

Southwestern TT Championship in Waco, Texas. *Clyde Earl*

# INDIAN PLANT SPACE DEMAND IS VERY HEAVY

### Inquiries Come From Garment Making Plants And Many Others

Although the Winchester Square plant of the Indian Motocycle Co. has been on the real estate market for only a month, there already has been enough demand for space there to insure filling the 426,000 square feet of floor space with tenants....

The five-story brick building is being offered for sale to a single buyer, however, rather than in small units....

The Indian Motocycle Co. does not expect to vacate the Winchester Square property until at least late summer....

*From* The Springfield Daily News, *April 15, 1947*

**Jack Colley and Chief, 1947**
Another of the last Chief racers was Jack Colley of Seattle, Washington, who won many area TT events. *Hap Jones collection*

*Chapter 7*

# 1948–1950

## *From Dream to Nightmare*

In early 1948, Ralph Rogers led a group of Indian executives on a multi-city tour to introduce the new vertical twins and singles to Indian dealers. During 1946 and 1947, registration of two-wheel motor vehicles had doubled to about 400,000 units, with the bulk of the increase made up of foreign lightweights. Accordingly, Rogers and his investors believed Indian would dominate the American motorcycle industry with the new models. The traveling team passed on its enthusiasm for Indian's future, and during the tour Indian doubled its number of registered dealers from 450 to about 900.

In the spring of 1948, Indian began relocating machinery and people to the new east Springfield one-story plant. The new vertical twins and singles weren't ready in time for the all-important spring sales season, due largely to the same problems with suppliers that had plagued Chief production. About 3,000 1948 Chiefs—one-fourth of the 1947 Chief production—kept the dealers in business while waiting for the promised lightweights.

July 1948 saw the first of the new lightweight motorcycles, the Arrow singles, go on sale in the Springfield Indian agency. In August, the new east Springfield plant officially opened, and in September *Business Week* magazine published an article about Indian's postwar program.

Unfortunately for Indian, in September the British government devalued the pound sterling from approximately $4 to about $3, which lowered the stateside retail prices of British motorcycles 20–25 percent. In November, Indian laid off 250 workers, leaving 800 still employed. Facing a disaster, Rogers went to England in December to work out a deal with J. Brockhouse and Company for a loan of $1.5 million.

In January 1949, Indian arranged for the Vincent-HRD Company to fabricate a prototype Indian-Vincent, consisting of a 1000cc Vincent overhead-valve V-twin engine mounted in a 1948 Chief chassis. This hybrid was a potential 1950 model that would continue for two or three years until a new big four-cylinder Indian could be on the market. Meanwhile, Indian's contract for CZ 125cc motorcycles had expired and the company was faced with a lack of lightweight motorcycles before CZ deliveries could be resumed.

In April 1949, as a condition of the $1.5 million Brockhouse loan, the Indian Motocycle Company agreed to the formation of a Brockhouse-managed company known as the Indian Sales Corporation. Hereafter, the Indian Motocycle Company existed as a supplier to Indian Sales, which in turn had the exclusive right to sell to Indian dealers so long as specified minimum amounts of Indian motorcycles were purchased by Indian Sales.

In November, the Indian Motocycle Company agreed to let Indian Sales and the dealer network sell the following British motorcycles: AJS, Douglas, Excelsior, Matchless, Norton, Royal Enfield, and Vincent. The Motocycle Company also decided to continue manufacture of Arrows and Scouts through the end of February 1950 at the rate of 250 (total) per month, for a total of 1,000 1950 model lightweights. These were to be discounted an additional 25 percent—sold at a loss, in other words. This would lower retail prices enough to ensure sales and, it was hoped, to raise enough capital to salvage the long-term future of the manufacturing company.

These heroic efforts proved insufficient to save Ralph Rogers' presidency. John Brockhouse had been working behind the scenes to convince the Indian Motocycle Company's major creditors that a management change was needed. The coup was completed at the January 1950 board meeting, with John Brockhouse replacing Rogers. The much maligned Rogers spent a lot of his own money, effort, and emotion on the Indian venture. In his absence, there is no assurance that Indian would have survived the turbulent postwar industrial era.

In February 1950, production approval was granted for 500 of the 1950 model year 500cc Warrior vertical twins and 500 1950 Chiefs. Production difficulties precluded converting the Chief to hand-clutch operation as promised to dealers, so dealers were permitted to cancel orders based on this feature. However, dealer

**Chief, 1948**
This advertising photo portrays the different motorcycling image sought by new Indian president Ralph Rogers. One can't help wondering if, in real life, a couple on a 1948 Chief ever rode on to a tennis court. Tennis was a relatively small-time sport then, and a status symbol of the affluent. *Hill/Bentley*

orders were expected to exceed production in any case.

In September, E. Paul du Pont passed away. As the man who kept Indian going through the Great Depression and World War II, he joins Rogers as an underappreciated figure in the Indian saga. Du Pont's passing closes the books on the du Pont papers, and thereafter Indian's business history is conveyed mainly in the Springfield press.

**Buddy Cosgrove and 101 Scout, circa 1948**
Still on the postwar hillclimbing scene were 101 Scouts, this one ridden by Buddy Cosgrove. *Hill/Bentley*

**Daytona Scout, Model 648, 1948**
A batch of about fifty Model 648 Daytona Scouts were built up from a combination of in-house parts and special-order parts. Jimmy Hill supervised the operation. *Dick Barth*

**Chief, 1948**
The 1948 Chiefs had a front-wheel speedometer drive, and a new, larger Stewart-Warner speedometer replaced the Corbin unit. The new instrument panel included a discharge light instead of an ammeter. This example was a prototype model, as indicated by the bulge on the front of the primary drive cover that housed the cushion drive sprocket. This feature was introduced on the 1950 production models. *Indian archives*

**Indian dealer, 1947**
Here, we see a well-dressed (and unknown) Indian dealer in 1947. *Earl*

**Ed Kretz, Sr., Ed Kretz, Jr., and Sport Scouts, 1948**
Few father and son teams have toured the professional AMA circuit. Ed Senior and Ed Junior were the most successful. *Ed Kretz, Sr.*

**Pikes Peak riders, 1948**
Bored? Try riding to the top of Pikes Peak on
New Year's Day. This group did the honors on
January 1, 1948. *Clyde Earl*

**Pikes Peak riders, 1948**
Leather flying caps were a popular way to keep
warm in those pre-helmet days. *Clyde Earl*

**Johnny Turnure and Chief, 1948**
Our hero atop Pikes Peak. *Clyde Earl*

**Max Bubeck and "Chout," 1948**
In June 1948, at Rosamond Dry Lake some 120 miles north of Los Angeles, Max Bubeck rode the Chase-Bubeck Chout 135.58mph, achieving the all-time fastest speed recorded for an unstreamlined Indian. The run was one-way, with speed somewhat reduced by a cross wind. *Max Bubeck*

**"Chout," 1948**
The forks were of Vard manufacture. The tires were 19x3.20in on the front and 18x4.00in on the rear. Twin Schebler carburetors handled the fuel. To reduce drag, the transmission housed no indirect gears and the motorcycle was run in high-gear only. Special cams were designed and built by Pop Shunk. *Max Bubeck*

**Butch Baer and Sport Scout, 1948**
Butch Baer, son of long-time Indian personality

Fritzie Baer, represents a typical Indian-mounted half-mile racer. *Bob Finn*

**Arrow, 1948**
A few production vertical twins and singles began to come off the assembly line in early 1948, in order to check out factory procedures and whet dealers' appetites for the new models. A few of the lightweights were taken to the Laconia 100-mile national championship. This example is an Arrow single. The men are Indian president Ralph Rogers on the left and Providence, Rhode Island Indian dealer Bill Gregson on the right. The boys are, left to right, Dean Gregson, Dick Rogers, and Bob Rogers. *Clyde Earl*

**Bob Waterfield and Scout, 1948**
Ralph Rogers launched an expensive publicity campaign for the new vertical twins and singles, featuring movie stars and other celebrities. Celebrities received new motorcycles as well as money for their modeling chores. Bob Waterfield, star quarterback of the Los Angeles Rams, took delivery of a vertical-twin Scout. *Hill/Bentley*

**Pretty gal, pretty Scout, 1948**
One of the professional models presumably shows the potential Indian buyer safe and easy to ride new verticals. *Hill/Bentley*

**Jane Russell, 1948**
Actress Jane Russell takes delivery of her Arrow from Santa Monica Indian dealer Harry Small. *Hill/Bentley*

176

# Color Gallery

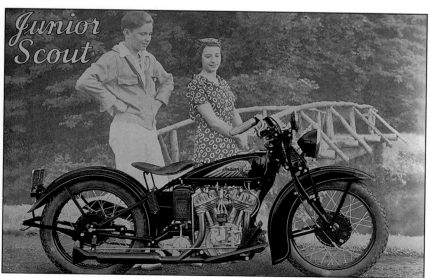

**Four prototype, 1938**
Catalog shot of the prototype 1938 Four. Production models had a different arrangement for the carburetor heater takeoff from the exhaust pipe. *Norman/Ellington*

**Junior Scout, 1938**
Catalog shot of the 1938 Junior Scout. *Norman/Ellington*

**Sport Scout, 1939**
Expert restorer Pete Sink displays his 1939 Sport
Scout. Restoration by Pete Sink.

**Sport Scout, 1939**
The first Indian offering of metallic paint was on the 1939 models. Sink's machine is dominated by Chinese red and metallic taupe.

**Sport Scout, 1939**
Closeup of the Sink 1939 Sport Scout.

**Four, 1939**
The historic 1939 Four on which Max Bubeck won the 500-mile 1947 Greenhorn Enduro. The motorcycle is fitted with the same Vard accessory front forks that he used then and which were quite popular in the late 1940s. Restoration by Max Bubeck.

**Thirty-Fifty, 1941**
The 1941 Thirty-Fifty, so named for its 30.50ci (nominal), 500cc displacement. The 1940 version had featured skirted fenders. The 1941 Thirty-Fifties were the last of the line. *Bob Finn*

**Sport Scout, 1941**
Also in its last *full* year of production was the 1941 Sport Scout. This was the only complete year of production with the spring frame. *Bob Finn*

**Chief, 1941**
The production models for 1941 had a chrome tank strip, but these preproduction photo models didn't get the treatment. *Bob Finn*

**Four, 1941**
One would be hard pressed to find a motorcycle with more beauty of line than the 1940 and 1941 Fours. This photo of a 1941 Four and the three previous photos were used in the 1941 sales catalog. *Bob Finn*

**Sport Scout, 1941**
This 1941 Sport Scout was accurately restored by Elmer Lower. Two-color finishes were a new offering on the 1941 models. Restoration by Elmer Lower.

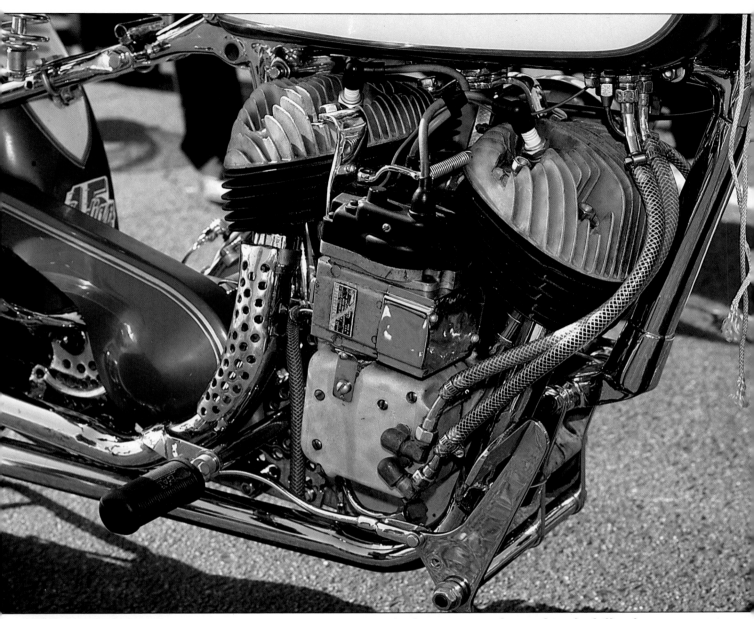

**Sport Scout, circa 1940**

Pick your year. Probably the most famous of surviving historical Indians is this Sport Scout campaigned by Ed Kretz from 1938 through the late-1940s. Born as a 1938 model, the motorcycle was later fitted with the large cylinders and heads that were introduced on the 1940 Sport Scouts. In the secret tradition of supposedly stock Class C racing, the machine had illegal powerplant mounting. The engine-transmission package was tilted forward, which raised the clutch hub area to provide additional ground clearance so important in dirt track left turns. Geared for long courses, Kretz's racer would reach about 114mph. Restoration by Ed Kretz, Sr., and Ed Kretz, Jr.

**Stark Leighty and Model 741, 1941**
Former Indian dealer Stark Leighty displays an
original unrestored Model 741 military model.

**Model 741, 1941**
Closeup of the Leighty Model
741. In late 1939 competitive
army testing, the Harley 45 had
the advantage in fender
clearance and electrical water
proofing. The 741 primary drive
and left-hand throttle were
among its strong points.

184

**Chief, 1947**
A 1947 Chief, resurrected from a basket case. This motorcycle provided the author with nine years of good riding and was sold only to finance an Indian Four. Restoration by Starklite Cycles.

**Chief, 1947**
Closeup of a typical late-1940s Chief. This 1947 model had the earlier-style ammeter.

**Arrow, 1949**
The 13ci Arrow single shared many components
with the 26ci Scout.

**Warrior TT, 1951**
A 1951 Warrior TT. Restoration by Chuck Rouse.

186

**Warrior TT, 1951**
Stylish tank trim on the 1951
Warrior TT.

**Warrior TT, 1951**
Closeup of the Warrior TT powerplant.

**Modified Sport Scout, 1992**
Craftsman Howard Wagner, and his hybrid custom featuring a Sport Scout motor in a vertical-twin frame. This idea was pursued by the Indian experimental department, as evidenced by a circa 1952 photo. Restoration by Howard Wagner.

**Rainbow Chief, 1942**
A popular Indian custom style is the Rainbow, created by John Polovik in 1942. This example belongs to dealer Bob Stark. Restoration by Bob Stark.

**Rainbow Chief, 1942**
Closeup of the Rainbow Chief
paintwork.

**Chief, 1967**
In 1967, the author purchased this Chief for $50, then sold it two years later in the same condition and for the same amount. There probably aren't many more Indians lying under straw in a barn, and if there are, be prepared to pay a four-figure sum for such a find.

**Dean Hensley and Munro Streamliner, 1992**
The late Dean Hensley, everybody's favorite guy, purchased and oversaw the restoration of the Bert Munro streamliner. *Gary Phelps*

**Indian riders, circa 1990**
A gathering of Indian riders at Bass Lake in Northern California. Happily, such scenes are continually enacted all over the world.

**Model 841, circa 1990**
From time to time, Model 841 shaft-drive ex-military machines have been civilianized.

**Six custom, 1980**
Representing the theme that Indian riders will go to any length to make their personal mount just right, here is the author aboard the Indian Six built by Herb Ottaway of Wichita, Kansas. Amazingly, an identical Indian Six was also built in Wichita by Bud Cox!

**Max Bubeck, 1987**
Another Indian theme (and the author's favorite one, at that): Don't just collect them, ride them! This was a roadside stop during Max Bubeck's 6,000-mile coast-to-coast ride in 1987. Max was a mere seventy years old at the time. The author covered half the distance with Max on the 1929 Model 101 seen here.

**History, 1981**
Known affectionately as the Wigwam, the old Indian factory on State Street was used from 1907 through early 1948, at which time production was moved to the one-story facilities in east Springfield. The Wigwam's highest annual production was about 32,000 units, in 1913; the lowest was 3,703, in 1933. President Rogers moved production to the east Springfield facilities as they promised greater efficiency for the planned large-scale production of the new lines of lightweight vertical twins and singles.

**"Cannonball" Baker, motorcycle queen, and Scout, 1948**
The old warhorse Cannonball Baker did his bit for Indian advertising by posing with the motorcycle queen . The verticals were more acceptable to shorter persons such as this young woman. Unfortunately, major technical problems beset the new lightweights, which would not stand up to long high-speed running, like Chiefs and the earlier Sport Scouts. Service manager Walt Brown related that he hated to go to work in the mornings because he knew awaiting him would be more wrecked engines returned by dealers. *Clyde Earl*

**Arrow, 1948**
One of the advertising themes was the suitability of the Arrow single for getting to and from work. Dealers stressed that the Arrow had sufficient power to avoid being threatened by fast-moving car traffic. The Arrows and Scouts used the same small magneto, the latter with a distributor. The magneto wasn't strong enough in the Scout application, however, resulting in difficult starting. You were OK if you lived on top of a steep hill, recalls one former Scout owner. *Hill/Bentley*

# NEW LOAN GIVES INDIAN CO. HERE STRONG STATUS

### New York Bank Puts Up $1,500,000 for Expansion Program

...The operation, financial structure and future of the firm has the confidence of the New York firm making the loan, sources said.... Rumors circulated here last week apparently stemmed from a report that a Springfield bank had turned down a loan to the firm. By word of mouth, the rumor was spread that Mr. Rogers had been removed as president. The Daily News spiked the rumor with a denial from Mr. Rogers.

A recent layoff at the plant was due to the slack season and officials said there is hope that the employees will be recalled next spring. However, new production methods at the plant are designed as the most modern for handling of the product and the company said at the time of the move to the new building that these methods would result in a decrease in manpower.

*From* The Springfield Daily News, *November 18, 1948*

**Modified Sport Scout, 1949**
The advent of the 1949 vertical twins and singles meant that it was legal to install the 1949 telescopic forks on earlier Sport Scout racers. *Hill/Bentley*

194

**Chief, 1949**
A few 1949 model Chiefs were assembled, with hand clutch and foot shift. Production of the 1949 Chiefs was halted almost before it began, in order to concentrate management efforts on continuing problems with the new series of overhead-valve singles and vertical twins.
The man with his hand on the seat is advertising manager Matt Keevers. *Clyde Earl*

# ROGERS DENIES LOSING CONTROL OVER INDIAN CO.
## *"Nothing to it,"* Motorcycle President Says, as Rumors Circulate

...Under the dynamic leadership of Rogers, Indian, in a postwar expansion program, has moved to a new stream-lined plant and has begun the manufacture of improved lightweight motorcycles.

Indian's postwar expansion program has involved heavy financial outlays, but recently the firm had reached a point where it was ready for mass production. Last summer, Rogers reported that Indian had a backlog of more than 10,000 machines ordered.

*From* The Springfield Daily News, *November 15, 1948*

**"Laconia" Scout, 1949**
One of a dozen Laconia 30.50ci (nominal), 500cc vertical-twin racers that Indian entered in the 1949 Laconia 100-mile national championship road race. Every vertical twin broke down! Magnetos accounted for most of the failures. Restoration by Bob Shingler.

**Warrior, 1950**
The 26.6ci, 436cc displacement of the vertical-twin Scout was never a plus with Americans, who were surrounded by 30.50ci, 500cc British motorcycles. So for 1950, the new 30.4ci, 498cc Warrior was offered alongside left-over Arrow singles and Scout vertical twins. Another change in the Warrior was its 1.5in higher seat. *Clyde Earl*

196

**Indian dealership, circa 1950**
Salvation of the Indian dealerships depended on sales of English motorcycles offered from late 1949. By mid-1950, it became difficult to find the Indian name on some Indian dealerships. More ominously, it even became difficult to find the marque for sale. Here, we see a long motorcycle lineup at an Indian dealership, but there isn't a single Indian in sight. *Clyde Earl*

# BRITISH IN CONTROL OF INDIAN CONCERNS AS ROGERS RESIGNS

*Top Official Since 1945 Is Succeeded By J. L. Brockhouse*
*Motorcycle Production To Be Continued in City Says Statement*

Ralph B. Rogers has resigned as president of the Indian Motocycle Co. and head of Indian Sales Corp., it was announced late yesterday, and it appears British interests are now in control of both organizations.

**Resigned Tuesday**

Rogers, who headed the motorcycle production concern since 1945 and was its top official in the sales organization since its formation in July of this year, tendered his resignation at a meeting of the board of directors in New York Tuesday. News of the resignation was given to plant employees yesterday afternoon and shortly afterward was made public.

...it was believed that Rogers had been forced out of the leadership of both companies by the British interests which put up the money to form the sales organization last summer, and that they have now taken over both the production and sales ends of the business.

**Another Chapter**

...Assumption of control of the companies by the British group marked another chapter in the turbulent financial history of the company.

**Started in 1889**

It had its origins in the Hendee Mfg. Co., incorporated in 1889, which was succeeded in 1910 by the Hendee Mfg. Co., incorporated in 1913. In 1913 the company sold its entire stock to the Harley Co., but took it back the following year in foreclosure proceedings....

**Took East Side Plant....**
**Hit Hard Blow**

The company suffered a hard blow during the summer when it was underbid by the Harley-Davidson Co. to supply a fleet of motorcycles to the Springfield Police Department. Although there was much criticism directed at the city purchasing agent for not buying the home product, he stoutly defended his duty to purchase the machines which met the specifications at the lowest price and the courts subsequently declined to issue an injunction restraining the award of the contract to Harley-Davidson.

Further difficulties were encountered during the summer and employees were asked to and did accept a 5 per cent pay cut in an endeavor to keep the company's head above financial waters."

[Author's note: The Harley company referred to in this article was a Springfield foundry. For awhile, the Harley company did all of Indian's foundry work, which led to an interesting advertisement!]

*From* The Springfield Daily News, *January 19, 1950*

**Chief, 1950**
The 1950 Indian Chiefs were the first built in quantity with telescopic forks. The new 80ci, 1300cc displacement was obtained by increasing the stroke from 4 7/16in to 4 13/16in. The front fender had less coverage and front-end droop than the earlier skirted-fender Chiefs. The cylindrical protrusion in the front part of the primary cover was the housing for the motor shock absorber, a coil spring, and ramp cam device. *Ian Campbell*

**Max Bubeck and Scout, 1950**
Max Bubeck, shortly after he won the 1950 Cactus Derby enduro in Southern California. The 200 miler ran from midnight to mid-morning at an average of 24mph. Bubeck's lights quit after ten minutes and he "hitch-hiked" lights from other riders. The course mixed deep sand, a combination of sand and small rocks called the Devil's Playground, narrow canyons, long steep hills, and high-speed running in occasional open spaces. Bubeck pulled out of a checkpoint in the early morning light, raced alongside a speeding freight train, and barely crossed the tracks before the train passed by. *Max Bubeck*

**Fred Marsh and Warrior TT, 1950**
Rider Fred Marsh, though in his fifties, continued to race Indians. The motorcycle was a 30.50ci, 500cc Warrior TT. *Bob Finn*

**Bobby Hill and Sport Scout, circa 1950**
Although Indians were fading away on the roads, a few Indian-mounted track stars were still emerging. Bobby Hill would soon win the coveted Number One plate. *Clyde Earl*

**Bobby Hill and Sport Scout, circa 1950**
In contrast to sales literature photos, most photos of dirt racers were taken from the infield area—left-side shots, in other words. This somewhat later shot of Bobby Hill shows a lighter non-Indian front fender. Speaking of lightness, builder-tuner Dick Gross pared down the Sport Scout until the complete machine, crated with spare wheel and tire, weighed less than the typical Harley-Davidson KR (post-1951) racer track-side! *Bobby Hill*

# Chapter 8

# 1951–Present

## *Slowdown, Shutdown, and Labeling*

The 1951 lineup included an unchanged Chief—the 1950 model had already ushered in telescopic forks. As well as the 500cc Warrior now in its second full year, there was the off-road version called the Warrior TT, for Tourist Trophy, which was launched as a late 1950 model. The vertical-twin Scout and single-cylinder Arrow were no more. In place of the Arrow was

**Brave, 1951**
For the 1951 season, Indian Sales Corporation imported the Indian Brave powered by a 15ci, 248cc Brockhouse-built side-valve single, coupled to a three-speed transmission. Technically, the machine was inferior to the overhead-valve Arrow that it replaced. However, its English origin and simpler specifications made it much cheaper to build, and cost was a critical factor at the low end of the market.
*Emmett Moore collection*

the Brave, a side-valve 250cc single designed and built in England by Brockhouse.

For 1952, Chief styling was changed and publicity photos also showed cosmetic changes to the Warrior. However, few if any of the 1952 Warriors went into production—none have surfaced in the collector market. Photos of the experimental shop during this period show a Sport Scout motor in a vertical-twin frame, so the idea of a revived Sport Scout hung around until the end. The sole American-made model in the 1953 lineup was the Chief; the last confirmed Chief production occurred in May 1953.

The number of 1950 through 1953 Chiefs is debatable. The Indian Motocycle Company records indicate that 500 Chiefs were planned for 1950. The late Emmett Moore, who hired on at Indian in 1953, recalled that 500 Chiefs were built in 1952 and 500 more in 1953. Taken together, the records and Moore's recollection suggest that the "magic number" was 500 for each year, 1950 through 1953, for a total of 2,000 telescopic-fork Chiefs. However, recollections, plans, and actual production figures are different matters. Canadian enthusiast Don Doody has made an extensive study of motor numbers and believes the total of 1952 and 1953 Chiefs was between 1,300 and 1,500. Regardless, the final stage of Indian Chief production was only a shadow of the great days at the Wigwam.

In 1954, Indian dealers offered only the Royal Enfield lineup, which were labeled as Royal Enfields. In July 1954, the Massachusetts state police ordered a fleet of Harley-Davidsons, ending a thirty-three-year run of Indian use.

From 1955 through 1959, Indian dealers offered badge-engineered "Indians," which were Royal Enfields labeled as Indians. The "Indian Enfields" didn't capture a strong following in the United States.

By 1960, Associated Motor Cycles (AMC) of England, builders of the English AJS and Matchless, had purchased the Indian Sales Corporation. Indian dealers became "Matchless-Indian" dealers, whose lineup consisted of Matchless motorcycles. These were given nicknames like Apache and Tomahawk in the sales catalogs, but the model names and the Indian label weren't displayed on the motorcycles.

To serve as the national distributorship, a large warehouse operation was opened in the Springfield area. Competition from Honda and other Japanese manufacturers quickly crippled Associated Motor Cycles. In July 1962, Associated closed the warehouse, terminated all American jobs, and sold the Matchless distribution rights to Joseph Berliner. Berliner never used the Indian name again.

The further evolution of the Indian trademark has been hotly debated in recent years. Continuity, a principle of trademark law, is questionable due to the apparent dormancy of the Indian Motocycle Company during the Royal Enfield and Matchless periods. Trademark law requires a trademark to indicate the source of the goods. Indian Motocycle records reveal that in 1950, the manufacturing company was concerned over losing the Indian trademark because Indian Sales was putting the Indian label on many products not routed through the motorcycle manufacturer.

Another trademark principle is that the holder of the trademark must challenge the unauthorized use of the trademark by other companies and individuals. For a generation, dozens of entrepreneurs have used Indian terminology and graphics in many ways, and without challenge. One could even argue that the Indian Motocycle Company abandoned its trademark rights in 1950, and that the Indian Sales Corporation never had a valid trademark.

The Indian trademark debate shows the intense feelings of Indian riders for their beloved marque. There may be room for another American-made motorcycle, but this question will be settled by issues of technical merit, style, price, distribution, and so on. The Indian name cannot stand for much when attached to a motorcycle having no historical connection to the *real* Indian motorcycles made from 1901 through 1953. Perhaps someday a congressional representative will take time off from raising taxes and increasing spending to draft a bill protecting historic trademarks from manipulation. Until then, I hope and believe that the passion for Indian motorcycles will stay focused where it belongs.

**Warrior, 1951**
For the 1951 season, the Warrior got a new two-color paint scheme on the fuel tank. *Hill/Bentley*

**The Wrecking Crew, circa 1952**
Here, we see two-thirds of the Indian "Wrecking Crew," which was so successful from 1950 through 1953. Left to right, they are: Ernie Beckman, Beckman's tuner/sponsor Art Hafer, Bobby Hill, and Hill's tuner/sponsor Dick Gross. *Finn*

*Left*
**Bobby and Nancy Hill and Sport Scout, 1951**
The girl, the motorcycle, and the Number One plate! What more could a guy ask? Bobby and Nancy Hill, following Bobby's win of the 1951 Springfield, Illinois, 25-mile National Championship. The win entitled him to use the Number One plate until the next Springfield twenty-five miler. Hill repeated his Springfield mastery in 1952, and fellow tribesman Bill Tuman won in 1953. Thus, Indian riders sported the Number One plate in 1952, 1953, and 1954, the latter year following halt of production. *Bobby Hill*

**The Wrecking Crew, circa 1952**
The rest of the Wrecking Crew is seen here, rider Bill Tuman and in the right margin of the photo, tuner/sponsor Erwin "Smitty" Smith. *Emmett Moore collection*

**Warrior, 1951**
This 1951 Warrior was restored
with period accessories.
Restoration by Elmer Lower.

**Indian factory, 1951**
Jimmy Hill, far left, supervises assembly of 1952
Warriors in the east Springfield complex. The total
of token 1952 Warrior (road model) production was
about eight. *Hill/Bentley*

**Vaughn Monroe and Warrior, 1951**
Vaughn Monroe accepts his annual Indian, a 30.50ci, 500cc Warrior. *Hill/Bentley*

**Police Special Warrior, 1952**
Former factory staffer Emmett Moore said this Police Warrior never went into production; however, Indian did advertise such a model.

The big-bucket Mesinger saddle, high handlebars, and footboards all were features likely to be popular with the cops. *Emmett Moore collection*

**Warrior prototype, 1952**
Scoop! A prototype 1952 Warrior. This is the first publicized photo of the prototype machine in this configuration. The cosmetics differ slightly from the final version intended for production. *Bob Finn*

**Warrior prototype, 1952**
The Chief generator is apparent. This rooftop shot was taken outside the Myrick Building sixth-floor penthouse used by the experimental department. *Bob Finn*

**Warrior prototype, 1952**
Records indicate that two experimental Warriors were completed and that an additional three machines were partially built from additional special parts. *Bob Finn*

**Warrior prototype, 1952**
From the rider's perspective, the prototype 1952
Warrior was more bulbous than its predecessors.
The large speedometer was similar (perhaps
identical) to that of the later Indian-badge Royal
Enfields, so plans for the Enfield connection
may have already been under way. The fuel tank
had a single center-mounted cap instead of the
double-cap appearance of the earlier vertical
twins. The wider Mesinger saddle and wider
fenders also gave a heavier look. Aside from the
larger, presumably more reliable, and definitely
more available Chief generator, did the total
motorcycle represent an improvement? One of
the charms—some say the *only* charm—of the
original vertical twins was their light weight,
about 300lb. That advantage appears to have been
sacrificed in the traditional American pattern of
adding weight without adding power. *Bob Finn*

**Warrior prototype, 1952**
The overdone front-end styling of the prototype
1952 Warrior. *Finn*

208

**Indian factory, 1952**
Lacking an upper fork panel behind the headlight, the motorcycle on the stand is an earlier version of the one shown before, or is perhaps a sister pilot model. Differences from the 1951 Warrior include the Chief generator under the seat, larger fenders used on the Police Warrior and the Torque Four, Mesinger full-pan saddle, enclosed saddle springs, Chief-style tubular lower rear fender brace, and Chief taillight. Equally interesting is the motorcycle on the stand in the background, which features a Sport Scout motor in a vertical-twin frame. Apparently, a revised Sport Scout was still being considered. *Bob Finn*

**Warrior, 1952**
Indian Sales Corporation ran this advertisement in the April 1952 issue of *Cycle*, and in the June issue of *Pow Wow*, the company's pocket-size magazine. This final prototype variant didn't have the gaudy chrome strips on the upper fork panel, but included a more complex paint scheme for the fuel tank. The road model 1952 Warrior prototype did not go into production. The rider is Bill Shultz, Indian's artist who did photo touchup work. The lady is office worker Elda (last name forgotten).

**Bobby Hill and Norton Manx, 1952**
The changeover of Indian dealerships to British lines is symbolized by this photo of Bobby Hill aboard his Number One Norton overhead-cam single after winning the 1952 Dodge City 200. Next to Hill was his tuner Dick Gross, and on the number thirty-nine Norton was third-place finisher Donald Fry. *Hill/Bentley*

**Dick Klamfoth and Norton Manx, 1952**
Indian's cloudy future was clearly written on the jersey of 1952 Daytona 200 winner Dick Klamfoth. This was Klamfoth's third Daytona 200 victory and coupled with Billy Mathews' 1950 win, and the 1947 and 1948 Sport Scout wins, the Indian Sales Corporation could claim five consecutive victories for its brands. This was good for Indian dealers, though it meant nothing as far as the continued manufacture of Indian motorcycles. *Bob Finn*

210

**Chief, 1952**
The 1952 and 1953 Chiefs featured a shorter front fender with a smaller skirt, upper fork panel, decal around the Indian tank script, engine cowling, low exhaust, Warrior muffler, and bench seat. *Bob Finn*

**Chief, 1952**
Representative of the last of the line was this 1952 Chief. The rear fender differed from earlier Chiefs in that the front lower section was flattened out in order to provide room for a larger battery on police models. *Bob Finn*

**Bob Finn and Chief, 1952–1953**
Bob Finn poses for a 1953 advertising layout. There were essentially no differences between the 1952 and 1953 Chiefs. *Bob Finn*

**Emmett Moore and Brave, 1952–1953**
Emmett Moore, cofounder of the Antique Motorcycle Club of America. After a long day at Indian Sales Corporation, Moore prepares to ride his Brave through the winter chill. Said Moore, "You're looking at the original Indian liar. I was so commissioned—believe me. All during the first half of '53, and maybe into the fall, we sent out bulletins which were just outrageous lies as to why there weren't any new Chiefs, and especially as to why there weren't any new Warriors. It got so bad that finally the dealers wouldn't believe us anymore." *Bob Finn*

212

# Emmett Moore On Indian's Final Production

"The last *big* batch of Chiefs was made in January of 'fifty-three, and I was there at the wake.... It's possible that [some] might have been assembled [as late as] May of 1953—it's possible that I don't remember the month. It might have gone into May of 1953—I'm not sure about that—but, anyway, those were the last of the Indian Chiefs assembled by Indian company at that time.... *Definitely* it was [no later than] the spring of 1953, and that was the end of Indian production.

"With regard to the question of what is known as the 1955 Chiefs for the New York City police department, I was just curious enough about this to call up my old friend Walt Brown, who was...manager in charge of experimental models....

"In 1953 he was assigned the job of expediting the assembly of the remaining 1953 models. He told me that the story about the 1955 Chiefs is a fable, that it never happened. He said that in 1953 they assembled seventy-five police models for New York City. They were the last models assembled at Indian. He said it's possible that one or two models might have been assembled later on, by an outside party such as a dealer, from parts. After they assembled the 1953 models at Indian, they were very short on parts and it just wasn't at all possible to assemble anymore motorcycles there. So you can put that down as a fable, because it came right from the horse's mouth, the man who supervised the assembly of the last Indians at that time."

**Indian factory, 1952–1953**
Perhaps half of the engine assembly staff is seen here. Said Emmett Moore, "In December of '52, the decision had been made to stop manufacturing motorcycles. I remember at their Christmas party, it was a sad Christmas party because there were 250 guys there that knew they were going to be laid off by next week." *Bob Finn*

**Indian Factory, 1952**
A corner of the engine shop is seen here in July
1952. *Finn*

**Indian factory, 1952–1953**
Final assembly was accomplished in the Myrick
building of downtown Springfield. Moore
related, "I remember when we were talking about
this new quantity of 500 for 1953. They went to
Linkert Carburetor. Linkert said, how many

*thousands* do you want? Indian said, 500; [and
Linkert said] forget it! That's why they went to
the Amal carburetor those last years. It wasn't
because it was better; they couldn't get a Linkert
carburetor for it." *Bob Finn*

**Indian factory, 1952–1953**
These are perhaps the last non-police Indians built in quantity. Myrick production-line manager Walt Brown surveys the lot, in a photo that was published in the June 1953 issue of the company publication *Pow Wow*. Of such photos, Emmett Moore said, "We were in the process of bamboozling the dealers as to future Indian plans. We didn't want to admit that there weren't to be anymore Indians, and we kept the dealers strung along with stories of production later on. Anytime there were machines sitting around like that, at that time, Bob [Finn] would go around and take pictures of them to back up our story. *Bob Finn*

**Grand finale, 1952**
More of what was probably the last large batch of American made Indians. *Finn*

**Indian factory, 1952–1953**
The wooden ceiling beams and flooring give this location away as the Wigwam. Motorcycle crates describe the contents as red police motorcycles with kilometric speedometers. Motorcycle serial numbers are marked on each crate, for example, "CS 6893" on the crate in the left foreground. Crates also state: "E378 14-8373 CASE #..." These numbers are apparently sales order numbers, with the "E" standing for export. The two crates on the right hold vertical twins, last built as 1952 models, so the Chiefs are probably 1952 models. *Bob Finn*

**Indian factory, 1952–1953**
Only three men were required to keep up with the polishing chores at this level of assembly in the Wigwam. Moore remembered, "But I was the official liar. I still got some of the bulletins here. I remember one of them said that due to the fact that the metal used in those machines was classified as strategic, we were unable to get it [he laughs]. Oh, I told all kinds of lies! Old Fred Stote, he was the president of the company [Indian Sales]; he was an Englishman. He thought that was creative." *Bob Finn*

## Indian factory, 1952–1953

The Wigwam operated as the supplies storehouse. Emmett Moore recalled, "I barely saw Indian production; barely saw it. They were really hurting because parts in such small quantities were costing so much to make. I can remember one little item. They had a dual seat on that model [Chief]. It had a little helper spring arrangement. The helper spring was engaged by sliding a little chuck up and down. I can remember because I had to purchase some of those chucks. [Note: Indian Motocycle Company was responsible for building stripped motorcycles; Indian Sales Corporation was responsible for buying and shipping accessories.] They originally cost something like twenty-five or thirty cents, when they were made in large quantities. But the 1952 quote was something like a dollar and a half apiece from Anderson Machine in Springfield."
*Bob Finn*

## Indian factory, 1952–1953

Parts were sent from the Wigwam to the Myrick building, and completed Chiefs were sent from the Myrick building back to the Wigwam for crating. Moore said, "And there was a day came, when I believe twenty-five or thirty Indian dealers who'd gotten together and descended on the factory en masse, and demanded to know, you know, demanded to see the president of the company, and why there weren't any more motorcycles and so on. I don't know what he told them. But that was the end of the lies. We couldn't tell any more lies. That was in '53."
*Bob Finn*

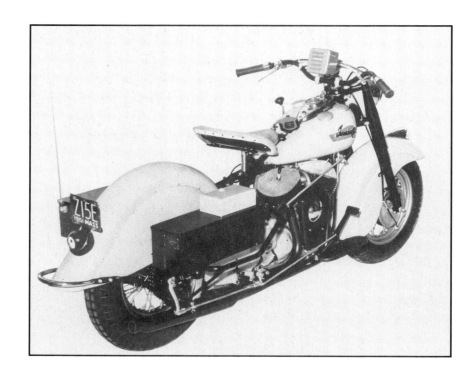

**Chief, 1952**
Indian kept building police
Chiefs until the very end, aided
by strong brand loyalty in some
departments. New York City
used Indians exclusively.
*Hill/Bentley*

**President Dwight Eisenhower and
Chief escort, 1952**
Every American president from William Howard
Taft in 1908 through Dwight Eisenhower in 1952,

was escorted at one time or another by Indian-
mounted police officers. Here, Ike campaigns in
Indian's hometown of Springfield. *Bob Finn*

218

**Patrol, 1953**

The last vertical twins built in quantity were Indian Patrol units. About fifty were built, most of which were sold to police departments. Win a trivia bet: These were the last Indians with standard right-hand shift. The shift lever can be seen beneath the saddle. *Bob Finn*

**Patrol, 1953**

A Borg-Warner clutch and transmission and a Crosley automobile differential were used on the Patrol. Colors offered were Indian red and gray. *Bob Finn*

**Ernie Beckman and Sport Scout, 1953**
Glory. This is Ernie Beckman, Sport Scout mounted, winning the 1953 Eight Mile National Championship at Williams Grove, Pennsylvania. This was Indian's last racing national championship. *Hill/Bentley*

# Indian Racing 1946 and Beyond

Indian began postwar Class C racing right where it had left the prewar game, on top. Ed Kretz won his fourth Langhorne 100 and Johnny Spiegelhoff won the Laconia 100. There was no Daytona 200, and the overall racing program was curtailed due to postwar readjustments.

However, from 1947 on, Harley-Davidson did better than Indian. Indian's growing financial problems prevented continuing Sport Scout production. Exceptional Indian moments were the 1947 and 1948 Daytona 200 titles of Spiegelhoff and Floyd Emde respectively. Emde's 1948 title was won on one of the last fifty Model 648 Daytona Scouts hand assembled by Jimmy Hill, Willard Wolfe, and one or two others. Kretz added to the 1948 luster by winning his fifth Langhorne 100 and the Riverside, California, 100-mile national TT.

In 1949, only one Indian rider, Ted Edwards, finished in the top twenty at the Daytona 200. At the Laconia 100, all twelve of the factory sponsored new vertical twins expired. Top riders switched to either Harley-Davidson like Ted Edwards, or to a British marque, like Ed Kretz going over to Triumph.

From 1950 through 1953, a trio of Sport Scout riders known as the Indian "Wrecking Crew" shared twelve national titles, although without any factory support. These riders and their sponsors/tuners were Bobby Hill and Dick Gross, Ernie Beckman and Art Hafer, and Bill Tuman and Erwin "Smitty" Smith. Hill won the 1951 and 1952 Springfield miles, and Tuman won the 1953 Springfield mile, giving them the Number One plate for the 1952 through 1954 seasons.

By this time, Harley-Davidson had established its dominance of the Class C game, aided by the 50 percent displacement handicap given to side-valve machines against foreign bikes. The formula no longer benefited Indian because of Sport Scout extinction. The Indian Sales Corp. and its Royal Enfield suppliers weren't up to the task of restoring racing glory under the Indian banner.

## State Police Unable to Buy Indian Cycles for First Time

*Mass. Constabulary Departs From 33-Year Precedent in Ordering Harley-DavidsonMachines*

...An official of the Indian Motorcycle Co. on Worthington St., said today that 'temporary' suspension of the production of domestic bikes precluded submitting bids for that order. He added, however, that Indian hopes to return to producing the famed local machine in the not too distant future....

*From* The Springfield Daily News, *July 12, 1954*

**Indian dealership, 1954**
Indian dealers who had not established strong sales of British motorcycles, faced rough going during 1954 when there were no new Indians on their floors. This was the Skinny Pierce agency in San Antonio, Texas. San Antonio had been a strong Indian city prior to the collapse of American production. Note the Royal Enfield in the foreground. A year later, the Enfields donned Indian trim. *Clyde Earl*

## INDIAN OUT TO RECAPTURE LOST MARKETS

*West Rejoins MotorcycleFirm For Dynamic National Sales Campaign*

Springfield's Indian Motocycle Co., within the next few weeks, will begin its most concentrated attempt in years to recapture its once vast domestic and police market, unveiling the most varied lines of motorcycles in its history.

Returning to the company as vice-president in charge of sales to head up this ambitious attempt that will mean more than 1000 new dealerships throughout the country to push sales of the new line, will be A. F. 'Al' West, who until May, 1953, was sales manager of the company he had been with since 1929.

...All of the bikes are being manufactured through a working agreement with the Royal Enfield Co. of Great Britain at the company plant in Redditch, England....

*From* The Springfield Daily News, *November 13, 1954*

**Indian (Royal Enfield) Tomahawk, 1955**
The 30.3ci, 496cc Tomahawk twin was a traditional mid-size British model known overseas originally as the Twin, and later as the Meteor Minor. In Britain and Europe 500cc machines were a staple, but the 500cc (nominal) capacity was not as popular for long, fast American roads, as were the 650cc and larger British models of various makes. *Bob Finn*

**Indian (Royal Enfield) Trailblazer, 1955**
The most popular of the Indian-badge Royal Enfields was the 42.2ci, 692cc Trailblazer, called the Super Meteor when flying its true Royal Enfield colors outside the United States. *Clyde Earl*

**Indian (Royal Enfield) Tomahawk, 1956**
The Tomahawks were also less profitable to
Royal Enfield than its larger twin. However, this
cubic capacity did qualify for AMA racing and
that may have been a factor leading to Indian
Sales' decision to import these models.
*Clyde Earl*

**Indian (Royal Enfield) Trailblazer, 1955**
Indian Sales Corporation tried to recover lost police business with the Trailblazer, modified with traditional Mesinger sprung saddle and footboards. This photo was taken atop the Myrick building. *Bob Finn*

**Indian (Royal Enfield) Fire Arrow, 1955**
Among the new badge-engineered Indians, the smallest was the 15.1ci, 248cc Fire Arrow. In overseas markets, the Royal Enfield equivalent was known as the Clipper. *Bob Finn*

224

**Indian (Royal Enfield) Woodsman, 1955**
Indian's off-road 30.4ci, 499cc Enfield was called the Woodsman. Overseas, the Royal Enfield 499cc singles were known as the 500 Bullet.
*Bob Finn*

**Fred Marsh and Indian (Royal Enfield) Woodsman, 1955**
Still plugging away, Fred Marsh, right, is seen here at the May 1955 race meet in Thompson, Connecticut. His mount was a Woodsman single.
*Fred Marsh*

**Indian (Royal Enfield) Woodsman, 1956**
A larger speedometer housing was provided on the 1956 Woodsman. *Bob Finn*

**Indian (Royal Enfield) Trailblazer, 1956**
This 1956 Trailblazer shows the popular accessories often fitted to these models. *Bob Finn*

**Indian (Royal Enfield) Apache, 1957**
The first significant styling change for the make-believe Indians was a chrome tank panel featured on the 1957 models. This 1957 Apache 700 was a slimmed-down version of the Trailblazer, giving customers a choice of two big vertical twins. *Clyde Earl*

**Indian show display, 1958**
The Indian Sales display of 1958 models at the Dodge City, Kansas, speed week. The range of imports was expanded for 1958 to include the little white job, a two-stroke Lance 150. This was a derivative of the 148cc Royal Enfield Prince. *Hill/Bentley*

**Indian (Royal Enfield) prototype Chief, 1958**
Called the Chief, this 42.2ci, 692 cc variant featured larger tires and fenders. Both police and pleasure Chiefs were offered. *Hill/Bentley*

**Dick Klamfoth, 1959**
During the summer of 1959, racing star Dick Klamfoth made several trips to Springfield to work with the Indian staff on developing the 30.3ci, 496cc Royal Enfield single. Power was about equal to a BSA Gold Star, which set the pace for racing singles in the United States; however, reliability never was adequate and Klamfoth's best outing was sixth place in the Laconia 100. One day, engineer Jimmy Hill was told to hurry and pack his bags for a trip to England. At last, Hill thought, he could get the needed factory modifications for the Royal Enfield single. Hill grabbed his extensive test notes, marked-up engineering drawings, and his suitcase, and jumped in the waiting car for a ride to the airport. In the car, Hill was told that the Royal Enfield connection was severed and that the new alliance would be with Associated Motor Cycles, builders of AJS and Matchless machines. Without comment, Hill lowered a window and threw out his accumulated Royal Enfield notes and drawings that had been years in the making. *Clyde Earl*

# Fading Away

A song of long ago proclaimed, "Old soldiers never die; they just fade away." So it was with Indian.

Outside the national championships circuit, the real American-built Indians could be seen racing into the late-1960s, though they were at last numbered by the handful and were the stuff of conversation. Hill-climbing Indians went further down the hunting trail, on into the 1980s, but hill-climbing by then wasn't the big sport it had been.

"Did you see that Indian at the race meet?" somebody would say, and the answer would be, "No. You mean there was one there! I haven't seen one of those since...." and thereupon the talk of middle-aged enthusiasts would be of good times in years past, when you didn't want to think about growing up.

**Matchless-Indian show display, 1960**
When the 1960 sales season arrived, the public was faced with a new twist. Associated Motor Cycles of England, builders of AJS and Matchless machines, bought the Indian name in order to gain broader market access in the United States. The new distributing company name was The Indian Company, and dealerships were called Matchless-Indian. Indian-style nicknames were given to the models, such as the 39.9ci, 646cc Apache twin in the left background, and the 30.4ci, 498cc Westerner single and 15.1ci, 248cc Arrow single. The "Indian" name was never put on the motorcycles, however. An oddity was the carry-over of unsold Royal Enfield-built Indian Chief vertical twins to be sold by Matchless dealers. One of these lame-duck Chiefs was in the right background. *Hill/Bentley*

# Motorcycle Firm Reaches
# End of Up and Down Trail

An abundant collection of yellowed clippings in *The Republican*'s files gives us some hint of the long struggle to keep The Indian Co. of Chicopee Falls alive.

## Will Close Soon

Announcement Saturday that the 61-year-old firm was finally breathing its last follows by only three years a brief period of extreme optimism when the Springfield firm broke ground for a new 20,000-square foot plant in the Massachusetts Industrial Park.

The Indian Co. was a champion of both lawmen and sportsmen from the days when the gasoline combustion engine was a mere infant.

But Saturday, Paul, now president, announced that the company, which has barely gotten settled in its new $165,000 plant in Chicopee Falls, was finished.

## Decision From England

The decision, Paul said, came from the company's English owners, Associated Motorcycles of London, England. because of the decline in the sale of motorcycles of all makes on the English home market.

Operations here, he said, will be combined with the Berliner Motor Corp. of Hasbrouck Heights, N.J., another division of the parent company.

The firm's 30 employees will be variously affected by the move. All sales personnel and some from the service department will join the New Jersey firm. Office employees will accompany the firm in the move.

Employees will receive notice and severance pay which will depend on the length of service with the company and the type of work performed, the notice said. State police roared after speeding motorists and gangsters get-away cars on Indian cycles for 33 years until 1954 when suddenly, there were no more new machines to be had from Indian.

...In 1959, Lawrence O. Paul, then executive vice-president, said Indian Co.'s line for 1959 was "the most extensive line of motorcycles in our 58-year history."

*From* The Springfield Republican, *July 29, 1962*

## Munro Special, circa 1967

Although Indians faded away in competition, with no certain definable last moment, it was only fitting that New Zealander Bert Munro be given the unofficial honor of Indian's last competition glory. Using an engine that started out as a 600cc side-valve Scout, and that grew into a 1000cc overhead-valve special, Munro rode his streamliner in several 1960s Bonneville speed trials. Homemade pistons were cast in the New Zealand beach sand; connecting rods were built by Munro from Caterpillar tractor axles; and many more tricks were devised by this persistent genius. His 1967 speed week two-way average of 183.586mph was the fastest of all motorcycles in attendance. His one-way run of 190.070mph over the Utah salt, was the highest speed ever recorded on an Indian. *Cycle World*

**Indian factory, 1952–1953**
What was it like to work in the Wigwam? Perhaps this photo conveys a little of the office atmosphere. The fan on top of the filing cabinet isn't working, and a window is open so it's a pleasant day. Through the windows we see a neighborhood home and an office building. Inside, we see the formality of white shirts and ties, and the ever-present plank flooring.
*Bob Finn*

# When A Business Fails

When a business fails, much more happens than is revealed in the final ledgers. The loss of a job, catastrophic at the time, is a loss you overcome. Later, maybe you even count yourself lucky that you were forced into another field that made you successful. But, people you've known for many years and seen several times a week or maybe every day, those familiar people become less so. Perhaps you'll see them again, now and then, when out shopping, but some will never again cross your path and years later you'll try to remember the name of that guy or gal that worked across from the water fountain or at the turret lathe on the far end of the shop. So it was at Indian, at the Wigwam, in East Springfield, in the Myrick Building, as each place played out its role, your turn came. You collected your personal things from your office or work station, picked up your last paycheck, and said your goodbyes. Good luck; great to know you; we'll meet up again. But the old life was gone and you moved on to new adventures and new workmates.

# Epilogue

## *The Wigwam was Alive*

This big brick building, this fortress, this Wigwam they called it, was once alive.

There were so many people that you bumped into each other. In the main shops lathes droned,

**Jake De Rosier family plot, 1992**
One likes to think that in the great beyond, old Jake De Rosier is racing around on a red Indian.

rivets popped, furnaces roared, motorcycles barked, and the art of lip reading was well developed. In the offices, could be heard the squeaking of the hardwood floors, a phenomenon the shop workers could sense only through the soles of their shoes. The shops got even, with the big drop forge hammers, which even if unheard inside the most recessed office, could be felt through the very ground on which the Wigwam sat.

There was more life to be sensed by touch. There was the rich feel of leather, the business-like touch of rubber, the frontier-evoking feel of wood over in the crating and shipping department. These things all had their own fragrances, together with the less pleasant but essential aroma of sweaty bodies hard at work.

There was the spring air that beckoned through open windows, tempting those inside to leave their places of duty. There was the heavy summer air that electric fans moved about, thereby helping the sweat to evaporate, giving a cooling effect in those pre-air-conditioned days. There was the crisp cold of the New England winter that somehow found paths around the edges of closed doors and windows—how the boys brazing frames were envied in the winter—how they suffered in the summer!

**Indian factory, 1981**

The Wigwam in 1981. This is the northwest-section on the State Street side, for a while occupied by King's department store. It was in the fourth floor office with the large semicircular windows, that early Indian president George Hendee charted the course of the world's largest motorcycle company. This portion of the Wigwam once housed the first vocational high school in the United States. Unfortunately, this most historic part of the Indian factory was torn down in 1985.

**Indian factory, 1981**
Two upstairs three-level bridges, covered by corrugated tin, connected the east and west halves of the Wigwam. Beneath, a rail line once started the far-flung journeys of crated Indians that were sent around the globe.

**Indian factory, 1981**
The ghosts of Hendee,
Hedstrom, and du Pont seem
to reside here.

*Left*
**Indian factory, 1981**
Interior of the eastern courtyard.

235

**Indian factory, 1981**
This was probably the one-time final motorcycle
assembly area.

**Max Bubeck and one-owner
1939 Four**
In a sense, Indian didn't fail.
How many products capture the
loyalty, even the love, of buyers
and hold that affection over fifty
years? This is the fiftieth
birthday party for Max Bubeck's
1939 Four, which he purchased
brand new. This 1939 Four is
still a practical and roadworthy
motorcycle, frequently ridden,
more than fifty years after its
creation.

236

*Appendix*

# Clubs, Dealers, and Museum

**Clubs**

All-American Indian Motorcycle Club, Inc.
Steven K. Gillis
3209 Melvin
Rochester Hills, MI 48063
    Established in 1965; publishes a quarterly newsletter; annual dues $10.

Antique Motorcycle Club of America (AMC)
Dick Winger, membership chairman
Box 333
Sweetster, IN 46987
    Established in 1954; publishes a quarterly magazine; provides contacts for any antique motorcycle need; especially valuable to collectors of older and rarer Indians for which dealer support is not available; eight or nine nationally sanctioned antique motorcycle shows per year; one or two nationally sanctioned road runs per year; many local chapter events; annual dues $20.

Indian Four Cylinder Club
Richard Davies
Rt. 2, Box 227
Rosedale, IN 47874
    Established in 1966; publishes a quarterly newsletter; annual meet in the Midwest; annual dues $15.

Indian Motorcycle Club of America
Box 1743
Perris, CA 93270
    Established in 1972 by Bob and Shorty Stark as an adjunct to their motorcycle business; publishes a monthly newsletter and a semi-annual booklet; many maintenance tips are offered; club discounts for purchases from the motorcycle shop; annual dues $25.

Laughing Indian Riders
Don Doody
4283 W. 10th
Vancouver, B.C., Canada V6R 2H5
    Established in 1984; publishes a quarterly newsletter emphasizing Indian history; much information on Indian personalities and current events in antique motorcycling; technical tips; annual dues $12.

Military Vehicle Collectors Club
Box 33697AM
Thornton, CO 80233
    Publishes a quarterly technical magazine; publishes an advertising journal bimonthly; annual dues $20 for US, $35 for foreign members.

101 Association Inc.
679 Riverside Ave.
Torrington, CT 06790
    Established in 1984; publishes a quarterly booklet with 101 Scout information not available elsewhere, including information applicable to other period Indians; annual meeting in conjunction with an AMC nationally sanctioned event; annual dues $15 for US and $22.50 for foreign members.

Vintage Motorcycle Club of Australia
The Secretary
167 Rosedale Rd.
St. Ives 2075 Australia
    Publishes a newsletter.

**Dealers**
This listing is for information purposes only and does not constitute an endorsement of any of the dealers.

American Indian Motorcycle Company
486 Rich Gulch Rd.
Mokelumme Hill, CA 95245
    Parts for Chiefs, Sport Scouts, and other models; catalog published.

Sam Avellino
240 Harris St.
Revere, MA 02151
    Royal Enfield and Enfield Indian parts.

Beard Machine, Inc.
18 Highland Ave.
Long Valley, NJ 07853
    New old-style bolts, nuts, and washers used from 1920s to 1950s.

Robert D. Beard
1241 Pinehurst Dr.
Fort Wayne, IN 46815
    Headlamps for Indians and other marques.

Bob's Indian Sales
RD#3, Box 3449
Etters, PA 17319
    Parts and service; uniquely knowledgeable in restoration details for late thirties and early forties models.

Bollenbach Engineering
296 Williams Pl.
East Dundee, IL 60118-2319
    Restorations, engine and transmission rebuilding, service.

Brownie's Indian Sales and Service
280 Broadway
Rensselaer, NY 12144

Max Bubeck
2274 Cardillo Ave.
Palm Springs, CA 92262
    Copper head gaskets for 1938–1942 Fours, laser cut, dealer discounts; Indian Four engine rebuilding, including modifications for modern road riding.

Woody Carson
1440 Lane Dr.
Placerville, CA 95667
    Cast brass carburetor covers for 101 Scout (not plated); cast brass Corbin speedometer head brackets #S195 (not plated).

Bill Clymer
3707 Otis Rd. S.E.
Cedar Rapids, IA 52401
    Early gas caps with primer, early ignition switch levers, reproduction lever-type headlight switch for 101 Scouts.

Coker Tire
1317 Chestnut St.
Box 72554
Chattanooga, TN 37407
    Tires for early American makes.

Coles Ignition & Mfg.
52 Legionnaire Dr.
Rochester, NY 14617
   Wiring harnesses.

Tony Conley
56 Main St.
Dresden, NY 14441
   Heli-arc welding to repair motorcycle
crankcases.

Dave's Motorcycle Parts
23106 Forest Ln.
Taylor, MI 48180

Dick and Lavera Davies
RR 2
Rosedale, IN 47874-9370
   Indian Four parts: magneto driveshaft and
bushing; gearshaft hub; coupling disc nuts;
generator driveshaft and bushing; steering
damper for leaf-spring forks; air cleaner
assembly for 1940–1942 (through 1951 on
Chiefs); air cleaner assembly for 1939 Four
(one year only); transmission mainshaft
bushings; cylinder base nuts; manifold nuts
for carburetor and exhaust; exhaust butterfly;
dash panel bolts, washers, and spacers; screws
for timing cover and oil pan; valve clevis nuts.

Decals
735 39th St.
Bettendorf, IA 52722
   Decals for Indians and other American
makes.

Dixie American Indian
Box 1602
Springfield, OH 45501
   Parts for Chiefs, Sport Scouts, and other
models; catalog published.

Dover Cycle Works
Rt. 1, Box 319, 39 West
Dover, OH 44622

Billy Doyle Battery Company, Inc.
4799 Irwindale
Waterford, MI 48328
   Indian motorcycle batteries (new).

John Eagles
17552 Delia Lane
Orange, CA 92669
   Repairs and restorations, specializing in
101 Scouts; magneto repair and overhaul.

M. F. Egan's Vintage Motorcycle
Box 738
Los Alamitos, CA 90720
   Parts and accessories for Indians and
Harley-Davidsons; catalog published.

Wally Enders
1118 Sherman St.
Bucyrus, OH 44820

Kevin Flanagan
Box 503
Rockaway, NJ 07866
   Compensator sprockets for pre-1950 Chiefs;
Indian script spark plugs, Indian amp gauges
for 1928–1934.

Allan Forbes
1 Coates Pl.
Edinburgh, Scotland EH3 7AA
   Reproduction handlebars for 101 Scouts
and other Indian models.

Paul V. George
2950 S.E. 52nd Ave.
Des Moines, IA 50320
   Rubber grips for 101 Scouts and others.

Larry Graham
Box 136
Hunt, TX 78204
   Royal Enfield and Enfield Indian parts.

Greenlight Inc.
1760 Monrovia
Costa Mesa, CA 92627
   Royal Enfield and Enfield Indian parts.

Jerry Greer's Indian Engineering
8400 Monroe Ave., Unit 3
Stanton, CA 90680
   Restorations, repairs, parts, literature,
motorcycle sales.

Gene Grimes
4006 Aspen Pl.
Oakland, CA 94602
   Fabricates battery boxes, generator belt
guards, and toolboxes for 101 Scouts.

Gene Harper
9350 W. Grandview Ave.
Arvada, CO 80002
   Reproduced parts for Splitdorf NS magneto
(101 Scouts): main cap, wire cap, rotor, and
brushes.

Howard Heilman
1605 Creek Hollow
Austin, TX 78754
   Leather saddle rebuilding for all American
makes.

Peter Heintz
775 Walnut Bend Rd.
Cordova, TN 38018
   Speedometer services.

The Hog Shop
26000 State Route 58 S.
Wellington, OH 44090
   Alemite grease fittings.

Indian Brothers
4118 N. Genese Rd.
Flint, MI 48506
   Parts and service.

Indian Country
Box 337
Ingleside, IL 60041
   Parts and service, Model 101 parts
advertised.

Indian Joe Martin's
Box 3156(L)
Chattanooga, TN 37404
   Parts; catalog published.

Indian Motocycle Restoration Co.
(formerly Island Restoration)
610 N. Queens Ave.
Lindenhurst, NY 11757
   Parts, sales, and service.

Indian Motorcycle Company of St. Louis
Box 44
Arnold, MO 63010
   Parts and service.

*Indian Motorcycle News*
Box 455
32606 Hartley St.
Elsinore, CA 92330
   Chief and Sport Scout parts; restorations;
catalog published.

Indian Motorcycle Supply, Inc.
Box 207
Sugar Grove, IL 60554
   Parts for Chiefs, Sport Scouts, and other
models; catalog published.

Indian Motorcycles Canada
Box 1
Marion Bridge, Nova Scotia,
Canada B0A 1PO
   Parts and service.

Indian Motor Works
Durango, CO
   Parts and services for all Indians.

Mike and Jessie Jacaruso
259 Sligo Rd.
Rollingford, NH 03869
   Leather and canvas products such as cable
covers.

Kenny's Indian Shop
73 McKinley Ave.
Warren, PA 16356
   Parts and service.

Kiwi Indian Parts
Box 7783, Dept. A
Riverside, CA 92513-7783
   Parts; catalog published.

Kjell-Ake Carlson
Ringvagen 7,
S-640 45 Kvicksund, Sweden
   Handlegrips, floormats, headlight lenses for
all Indian and other American makes,
1913–1934.

Kokesh Motorcycle Accessories
6529 University Ave. N.E.
Fridley, MN 55432
   Linkert carburetor brass floats, needles, and
seats.

L&W Sidecars
RD 3, Box 1106
Duncannon, PA 17020
   Parts and service, many 101 Scout parts,
reproduction Sweetheart sidecar for 101.

Roger Long
11107 Eller
Fishers, IN 46038
   Reproduction flag holders that fit on
headlights; luggage racks with fender clip
mounts.

Conrad Lytle
122 Essex Ave.
Glen Ridge, NJ 07028
   New and rebuilt Indian petcocks, Part
#35B93X.

Marietta Vintage Cycle
680 Applewood Lane
Marietta, GA 30064
   Indian solo and dual seats recovered; original style saddlebags, mud flaps, and kidney
belts.

Robert B. McClean
2411 Middle Rd.
Davenport, IA 52803
    Decals for all Indians and other American makes.

Chuck Myles
Box 150
Sloansville, NY 12160
    Parts and service for all Indians, specializing in Chiefs and Sport Scouts; catalog published.

Osprey Ltd.
PO Box 68
Cummington, MA 01026
    Indian saddlebags.

Bill Patt
RD 7064
Reading, PA 19606
    Oil pump testing nozzle and carburetor venturi.

Rocky's Antique Parts
6813 Highmill Ave.
Massillon, OH 44646
    Parts; catalog published.

Doc Schuster
24183 Nichols Rd.
Monroe, OR 97456
    Early (large-diameter) speedometer cables, inner and outer.

Fred Schutt
5321 Burney Lane
Kerrville, TX 78028
    New repro intake and exhaust manifolds for 1940–1942 Fours; new repro center stand.

The Shop
6541 Ventura Blvd.
Ventura, CA 93006
    Parts and service for most Indians.

Starklite Cycle
Parts Department
21230 Gold Valley Rd.
Perris, CA 93270
    Parts for Chiefs, Sport Scouts, verticals, and other models; catalog published.

Starklite Cycle
Service Department
1101H Ash
Fullerton, CA 92631
    Walk-in service for most Indians; specializing in Chief repair and complete restorations; gasoline tank repair; all Indian repair and restoration jobs accepted; common maintenance parts in stock.

Ed Strain
400 2nd Ave. N.E.
St. Petersburg, FL 33701
    Magneto parts, repairs, sales of used and rebuilt magnetos.

Herb Sweet's Indians
Chatequgay, NY 12920
    Parts and service.

Timmerman's
Argentinische Allee 33, 1000
Berlin 37, Germany
    Many parts for 101 Scouts and other Indians of the era.

Calvin E. Wahl
131 Fuhrman Ave.
Ramsey, NJ 07446
    Stocks 101 Scout parts: metal footboards, rubber footboard covers, footboard cleats.

Randy Walker
7 S. Maple St.
Brookfield, MA 01506
    Indian 1931 muffler and tail piece.

Waxahachie Emporium
InterUrban Court
116A North College
Waxahachie, TX 75165
    Chief, Sport Scout, and verticals parts.

Ernie Webb
5420 Sharon View Rd.
Charlotte, NC 28226
    Silver plating for headlight reflectors; remanufactured generator brackets for Model GAS 4102 Auto Lite generator (1931 101 Scout); 1930 and later remanufactured headlights.

Ted Williams
1685 Green Valley Rd.
Yuba City, CA 95991
    Parts, including stroker kits for Chiefs.

Mort Wood
14943 York Rd.
Sparks, MD 21152
    Complete motorcycles, parts, and literature.

Stephen Wright
503 Delaware, Apt. B
Huntington Beach, CA 92648
    Spokes for early American motorcycles.

Jake Wurtzenberger
RR 2, Box 39A
New Ulm, MN 56073
    Parts for Chiefs, Sport Scouts, Fours, 101 Scouts, and Junior Scouts.

G. L. Yarocki Co.
679 Riverside Ave.
Torrington, CT 06790
    Parts and information on Model 101 Scouts, reprints of factory literature and magazine articles dealing with all American makes; repair and alignment of 101 Scout frames and forks; 1928–1931 101 exhaust systems, 101 wiring kits; catalog published.

Ken Young & Son Motocycles
1676 Hayes Ave.
Long Beach, CA 90813
    Indian Four parts, services, and complete restorations.

**Museum**
Indian Motocycle Museum
33 Hendee St.
Springfield, MA 01104
    The museum is located in part of the east Springfield Indian works purchased by the company prior to World War I, sold, then purchased after World War II by the Ralph Rogers group to manufacture the vertical twins and singles. Open year-round, the museum is operated by Charles and Esta Manthos. Featured are the hand tools used by Oscar Hedstrom to construct the original Indian prototype, as well as some personal effects of George Hendee. Also on display are trophies won by Hedstrom at early events such as the 1906 Ormond Beach speed trials. A prototype Indian car and a number of Indian motorcycles are on exhibit as well. A museum highlight is the rotating display of Indian archives photographs, drawn from the largest collection in the world. The museum organized and perpetuates the Indian Motocycle Hall of Fame, which is another museum focal point. The museum hosts an annual Indian Day on the third Sunday of July.

# Index